BIO-ETHICS AND BELIEF

*The Church derives religious and moral
principles from the deposit of God's Word
which it safeguards, but it does not
always have a ready answer to particular
questions. It desires to combine the
light of revelation with human expertise,
so that the way on which humanity
has entered may be illuminated.*

THE SECOND VATICAN COUNCIL
PASTORAL CONSTITUTION ON THE CHURCH
IN THE MODERN WORLD,
§ 33.

Bio-ethics and Belief

*Religion and Medicine
in Dialogue*

John Mahoney

Sheed & Ward
London

ISBN 0 7220 1319 1

Nihil obstat Brendan Soane, BSc, PHD, STL, Censor. *Imprimatur* Ralph Brown, Vicar General, Westminster, 7th March 1984.

Published in Great Britain in 1984 by
Sheed & Ward Limited,
2, Creechurch Lane,
London, EC3A 5AQ

Book production Bill Ireson
Filmset by Fakenham Photosetting Ltd, Fakenham, Norfolk
Printed and bound by A. Wheaton & Co. Ltd, Exeter, Devon

To my students

Contents

Introduction

Moral issues arising from the development and practice of medicine have for long had a particular attraction for Roman Catholic moral theology; and on occasion this careful tradition has even drawn the accusation of concentrating on personal, or individual, ethics to the neglect of issues which have a greater social dimension and importance. In recent years, however, the remarkable advances which have taken place in medical science and technique, and the growing and widespread availability of such advances, have greatly increased the real and potential impact of medicine not only on many more individuals but also on society as a whole, as it contemplates the management and control of human life from its conception to its dying and at various intervening critical stages.

Such increase in medical resources, and in the moral issues attendant upon them, is reflected in the concentration of attention which has given birth to the newly-described science of bio-ethics, which the *Encyclopedia of Bioethics* explains as 'a composite term derived from the Greek words *bios* (life) and *ēthikē* (ethics). It can be defined as the systematic study of human conduct in the area of the life sciences and health care, insofar as this conduct is examined in the light of moral values and principles'.[1] The chapters which follow are devoted, then, to bio-ethics, but not simply from the standpoint of moral values and principles, although these latter occupy a large part of the study. The approach is more fundamentally undertaken from the standpoint of religious belief, and specifically of Christian belief as this has traditionally inspired the discipline of moral theology. It is therefore as a believing Christian that I have approached this work, writing from within the Roman Catholic moral tradition, but also reflecting upon that tradition and its contemporary positions. However, the purpose

9

of this work is not to dogmatise, but to dialogue; and specifically to explore not only what religious belief has to offer to medicine but also, as of equal importance, what contemporary medicine has to offer to religious belief, in the hope that such exchange will be to their mutual enrichment. My hope is also that others who do not share the Roman Catholic expression of Christian beliefs and Christian morality will nevertheless find in the following pages religious and ethical considerations which make appeal much more to reason than to authority. It is on that account that references to authorities and to the literature on the various questions considered have been kept to an absolute minimum, and restricted to identifying passages used in the text. The aim has been to permit the arguments to speak for themselves without that support which those knowledgeable in the field would find unnecessary and those not so conversant would find distracting.

The actual format of this work follows that of a course of lectures which I had the honour of being invited to deliver in February 1983, at the Catholic Chaplaincy of the University of Glasgow, and I am happy to acknowledge my gratitude to the Chaplain, The Rev Michael J. Conway, BA, MSc, and his colleagues, both for the invitation and for the warmth of their welcome on that occasion. The contents have been considerably expanded, partly in the light of the stimulating discussion which followed each lecture, and partly to incorporate more detailed and sometimes more developed aspects of the subject. I am grateful also to my colleagues, Rev John Russell, SJ and Rev G. J. Hughes, SJ, of Heythrop College, London, for comments made on this work in its final draft. And I am particularly grateful to Dr Michael Hobart for having checked the work for any technical inaccuracies. Such faults, whether of fact or of reasoning, as may remain are entirely my own.

A central section of my study is Chapter 3, *The Beginning of Life*, to which various considerations treated in earlier chapters will point forward. Rather than begin with that fundamental issue, I have preferred to deal first with various contemporary issues which serve to highlight its importance, but I hope the reader will bear in mind in these early chapters that many of their conclusions may well be qualified by the position one adopts on the beginning of life for the human individual.

Human Fertility Control

Of the various remarkable achievements and advances in medicine in the past half-century, many can be seen as important developments in the discipline, and others as revolutionary turning-points for human society. The break-throughs, such as the discovery of penicillin, kidney and heart transplants, intensive care and laser surgery, may all, of course, be seen as possessing social implications in terms of improving the individual lives of countless individuals. Other advances, however, may be seen as offering completely new options to the human race, and of opening up new social horizons, such as the discovery of DNA and the expanding field of microbiology, with its implications for genetic manipulation, human and otherwise, giving man a biological power comparable to the nuclear energy generated by the splitting of the atom. Another, which may not be far from us, will be the capacity to determine in advance the sex of children and hence of future generations, with all the social repercussions which that will entail. At present the most sensational, and the most debated, revolutionary turning-point which the advance of medical science has offered to society is the developing technique of *in-vitro* fertilisation, whose applications and implications for society are being urgently considered by various professionally sponsored working parties, and particularly by the interdisciplinary Government Committee of Enquiry into Human Fertilisation. This newly acquired expertise in controlling human fertilisation is one which poses important questions for religious belief, and equally stimulates belief to address to it various considerations relating to human life and relationships in society. The purpose of this opening chapter is to engage both belief and medicine in a dialogue concentrated on the subject of human control of fertilisation.

It may be helpful at the outset to introduce a distinction between positive and negative control of human fertilisation, and to consider the former as covering procedures aimed at achieving fertilisation in a variety of medical and personal situations. By contrast, negative control considers the variety of contraceptive techniques directed towards preventing human fertilisation. One objection to such a distinction may be that it appears to overlook the question of how certain techniques commonly termed contraceptive may achieve their effect, such as intra-uterine devices and various types of post-coital pills, but if there is ambiguity in this area it centres on whether certain techniques should more properly and accurately be termed abortifacient than contraceptive, and this we shall consider later. For the present we shall concentrate on positive methods of achieving fertilisation, with the possible consequence that consideration of this area may also throw light on the whole vexed question of contraception.

It was in 1951 that Roman Catholic moral teaching first officially took note of human *in-vitro* fertilisation, in an address of Pope Pius XII which took up the condemnation he had directed two years previously against human artificial insemination, even by the husband, and which he was to repeat in 1965 in a speech to participants at the World Congress on Fertility and Sterility.[1] In 1978, when the first completely successful 'test-tube baby', Louise Brown, was safely delivered, such official reaction as was expressed in the Roman Catholic Church came from a few individual bishops in varying degrees of favour (including the Patriarch of Venice, later Pope John Paul I, who was reported as being delighted for the mother), with other bishops objecting to what they considered to be at variance with the Church's moral teaching. No statement on the subject has been made by the Vatican, and the present situation may be usefully compared with offical Church teaching on the morality of transplantation of organs such as the kidney from living donors, a practice which many thought condemned by Pope Pius XII in his day, but which appears to have become since then increasingly, if tacitly, countenanced in Roman Catholic moral thinking, despite the continued disapproval of various individuals.

In objecting to artificial insemination, even by the husband,

and to *in-vitro* fertilisation, even using material obtained exclusively from husband and wife, Pope Pius XII appealed to two fundamental considerations which may still today express at least some of the misgivings felt in the minds of those who react adversely to these new methods of fertilisation, quite irrespective of the various ways in which they can be applied, and which we shall examine later. The technique itself appeared to him to offend on two counts: that the semen used is obtained by masturbation, a practice which has long been considered morally reprehensible; and that the fertilisation procedure itself disrupts the intrinsic relationship between loving marital intercourse and the emergence of a new human being as the expression of such love. Reflection on these two considerations, however, in the context of positive control of human fertilisation, reveals certain weaknesses which call for consideration.

Pius XII's moral objection to masturbation as a method for providing semen was based on a philosophical consideration of the human reproductive system and organs and what he considered their obvious and inherent purpose, that of contributing to the production of a new human individual. This being so, the wrongness of masturbation lay in its 'frustrating' this purpose, in setting in train the male reproductive potential in circumstances which clearly did not favour its achieving its effect. Masturbation was a reproductive contradiction, an action which, as the 1976 Vatican Declaration on Sexual Ethics explained, 'essentially contradicts' the purpose of human reproductive organs. It may be noted, of course, that all reference to the sexual faculty as designed with an inherent and built-in purpose, that of procreation, relies heavily on religious belief in a Creator who has so fashioned man that from his very constitution he is able to deduce that the God who made him wishes him to comport himself in certain ways by respecting the data of human bodily existence. In the area of sexual conduct this would include a recognition of God's purpose in creating man with sexual characteristics and a respect for their divinely-ordained nature and function, such that any behaviour at variance with that nature and purpose would not only contravene the wishes and intentions of the Creator but would at the same time be a misuse of man's sexual powers.

Such a traditionally Roman Catholic expression of 'natural law' has come under considerable fire in recent years, largely, it is interesting to note, in connection with the conclusions concerning contraception to which it appears to lead. Even for the believer reflecting within a Christian context, it may be considered an unduly minute application of a form of argumentation from the divine purpose in creation which is more compelling in its more general conclusions relating to human individuals as a whole. But even within the particular argumentation against masturbation, to which Pius XII appealed, and which considers such behaviour in general as morally wrong on the grounds that it actuates man's sexuality to no good reproductive purpose, what this line of argument does not take into account is that in some circumstances the practice is resorted to precisely to achieve procreation and to correct the process of human reproduction in cases where it has repeatedly failed. It is difficult also to avoid the conclusion that, had another term than 'masturbation' been used to describe such behaviour in a context of attempting to achieve human fertilisation, then the moral reprobation of the procedure on philosophical grounds would not appear to be so strong or convincing. The term itself, it is sometimes suggested, may derive from a Latin phrase meaning manual defilement, and without going into the question of religious feelings deeply connected with matters of ritual hygiene and cleanliness, there can be no doubt that the word bears an aura of sexual shame connected with the practice being resorted to for sexual pleasure and relief in solitary circumstances. The intensity of pleasure associated with male emission in privacy is at least as operative in all condemnation of masturbation as any more philosophical considerations, and contributes an element of emotional distaste to any verdict passed on the practice even when it is not self-centred. It is, in fact, the centring of the action which gives it moral significance as an expression of sexuality. Human sexuality is essentially relational and interpersonal, so much so that the major ethical problems concerning contemporary sexual behaviour can be seen as situated in the connections between sexual activity and love, and between sexual love and marriage. This being so, the disordered element in masturbation lies in its being a form of sexual behaviour which denies the interpersonal dimension of human sexuality and turns it in on itself as a form of self-love. But if this is the case, then what is termed masturbation to produce male semen is anything but the exercise of self-directed love. It is not undertaken for its pleasurable accompaniment, and it is essentially other-directed, orientated towards the production of a new human being who will literally embody the generous love between husband and wife.

The fundamental objections, then, which have been or might be put to the action of masturbation in general are its biological futility and its emotional futility. But neither of these considerations is applicable in the cases which we have been considering, where the production of semen is directed towards reproduction and is a physical expression of marital and parental love. It might be objected, however, that this and other stages of artifical insemination or *in-vitro* fertilisation cannot be appropriate expressions of married love, or suitable 'carriers' of the interpersonal love between husband and wife. And this brings us to the second of Pius XII's arguments against these medical techniques for producing a child, that they divorce the conception of the child from its normal and natural context of loving marital intercourse and so prevent it from being the fruit of the totally expressed love of husband and wife. It is interesting to note that essentially the same line of argument has been recently expressed more succinctly and in more explicitly religious terms by the Archbishop of Melbourne, responding to developments in Australia where work on *in-vitro* fertilisation is being actively pursued. One must begin, he argues, from 'the fundamental principle: God has bound the transmission of human life to the conjugal sex act ... [I]f science seeks to exclude or substitute the marital act, the scientific action is not licit'.[2]

There are two difficulties about this argument, with its latent appeal to the teaching of Jesus on divorce that what God has joined together man may not put asunder. The first is a difficulty from which many arguments claiming the weight of 'natural law' suffer, that because things have always been thus, this is the way in which they must continue to be. It makes a silent transposition from the factual truth that in the past there has been only one way of achieving certain effects to a moral truth that for the future, despite the development of alternatives, there can be only one morally permissible way to achieve those effects. Frequently such a line of thought springs from a mentality which will prefer to canonise the past and the familiar than to explore the unknown and the future; and as such it is, of course, profoundly at variance with the scientific mentality and, it may be added, with the general modern mentality which feels increasingly at home with change and does not consider it necessarily disquieting. The more static mentality will tend to think of the spontaneous and the customary way as more 'natural' and more characteristically human than the 'artificial', the calculated and the contrived, not to mention the clinical. And in this it is profoundly mistaken, for the characteristically human qualities are intelligent control of the environment coupled with respect, and simple human ingenuity in finding means to ends. In more religious terms, the difference is one between the passive acceptance of God's gifts and finding in them the challenge of active stewardship, so that the ultimate religious defence for any status quo, including the biological or the human, cannot be an appeal to the doctrine of creation as the divinely guaranteed blueprint for human nature and human living for all time. If that doctrine is to be appealed to, it is more in terms of the human values which man owes ultimately to God and the ways in which those values may be enhanced or endangered by human developments and activities. Moreover, so static a view of things is ill-equipped to handle the process of human evolution, whether before the appearance of man or since that time, or to accept that the bodily functions which the human species has inherited from its forebears may now be used in more characteristically human and intelligent ways, and be called upon to express relationships not just between individuals but between persons.

Within the present context, although it may also have implications for contraception, this line of thinking leads one to enquire why it is that only loving marital intercourse may be the context and the cause of human procreation. To this question no answer appears to be forthcoming, except to reassert it as a God-given datum which appears to be claimed as in some sense self-evident. Such an objection to artificial insemination by the husband and to *in-vitro* fertilisation simply discounts the possibility that other actions between husband and wife can be, in the circumstances, equally expressive of their mutual love and equally fruitful. The Roman Catholic Church has taught that at times, such as sickness or pregnancy, abstinence can be at least as equally loving as marital relations. It is clear that the production of a child should be expressive of the loving personal interchange between husband and wife, and not just an impersonal, clinical contribution by each of the ingredients required for conception; and it was this consideration which led Pope Pius XII to warn against 'turning the sanctuary of the family into nothing more than a biological laboratory'. But it is equally clear that the frustrations of childless couples and all the disruption and inconveniences entailed by clinical procedures for artificial insemination and *in-vitro* fertilisation can also be expressions of deep mutual love and of a shared longing to give each other a child as the fruit of their married life and love expressed in manifold ways from day to day. It is one thing to state that a child must be the expression of marital loving actions, but quite another to state that only through the marital act itself may loving union be expressed and made effective. And if science can now bring to birth this living expression of the love between husband and wife which would otherwise simply not exist, this too, it would appear, must be seen as part of the Creator's loving plan for all his children.

In the absence of more cogent objections, then, we may conclude that there is nothing morally wrong in principle about resorting to artificial insemination by the husband or to *in-vitro* fertilisation within a marriage when the genetic material is provided by husband and wife. What this tells us, however, is that in certain circumstances the application of these procedures is morally legitimate and even desirable. The procedures themselves are neither moral nor immoral, like so many other scientific and medical techniques or developments. The process of generating nuclear power, for instance, which is such a controversial issue today, is in itself morally neutral, and receives its moral tone or coloration from the uses to which it is applied, whether constructively to meet the energy needs of man or destructively to blot out whole areas of the globe with their inhabitants. Similarly, as a solution to problems of infertility in a marriage, the application of artificial insemination

17

and *in-vitro* fertilisation procedures utilising husband-semen and wife-ovum appears a legitimate and laudable procedure, but new problems and considerations arise when the material drawn upon is not specific to the marriage partners, but is donated from an outside source, whether male semen, as in artificial insemination by a donor, or female ovum, as in egg transfer from a donor or in surrogate motherhood.

To what is seen as the intrusion of a third party into a marriage as a means of remedying its infertility the Christian, and particularly the Roman Catholic, response has been on the whole uniformly hostile. Apart from social and legal considerations pertaining to secrecy of true parentage and even falsification of public documents and records, and apart also from the charge that the so-far-anonymous donor is either unwilling or unable to exercise parental responsibility towards the child produced, the basic religious objection to such intervention of a third party is that it trespasses upon the covenant and exclusive relationship between husband and wife who are, as Genesis describes it, 'one flesh', as well as intruding into the parent–child relationship of the family. As evidence and confirmation of this much is often made in some arguments of the biological imbalance introduced into the parent–child relationship when only the mother or, in egg transfer, the father is completely a parent. Much is also made of the resultant stress between husband and wife when a child who ideally should be the fruit and the physical embodiment of their love and union can constitute rather a perpetual reproach of personal inadequacy. It should be noted, however, that if attention is concentrated on this evidence alone, as the harmful personal and interpersonal consequences which are predicted as the inevitable result of donor contribution, then such consequences are in principle verifiable by follow-up studies of families which are the result of such procedures. It might, for instance, turn out that not all marital and parental relationships are undermined in such cases. It is also worth noting that, if biological and relational imbalance between the genetic parent and the social parent is urged as the major objection, then there is a rather close parallel in the case of second marriages to which one partner may bring children of a previous marriage, of whom the other partner would be only the step-father or step-mother. Despite the popular image of cruel step-parents, similar perhaps to that of mothers-in-law, there are many instances of successful and loving, if difficult, adjustment to such circumstances.

What these considerations lead to is a warning, if not a reproof, which belief can receive from science, with its concentration on strict accuracy in verifying hypotheses and on precise proofs and arguments, not to translate its present revulsion automatically into unproven predictions of future disaster. If the application of some new procedure is convicted of wrongness because of the harmful consequences to which it will lead, the accuracy of such prediction can be checked, and perhaps even the possibly harmful consequences can be avoided or controlled by some other means. To appeal to consequences in cases of artificial insemination by a donor, and of egg transfer from a donor, is implicitly, on pain of dishonesty, to submit to a testing of such consequences, and to the possibility of being proved wrong. It may be, however, that in such cases of predicting disastrous consequences from contemplated behaviour there is a hidden step in the argument, which is taken for granted by the believer and not suspected or adverted to by the more empirical scientist. It is the conclusion that if something is known to be morally wrong on grounds other than the consequences to which it will lead, then it is ipso facto harmful and this will inevitably show itself in the results of the behaviour. Prediction here partakes more of an implicit belief that the sinner cannot enjoy a happy life, than of a scientific projection into the future. And in many instances it is simply disproved by the facts, to the bafflement of some believers who may then resort to a difference between leading a happy and enjoyable life and being 'really' happy, in an attempt to deny or undermine the facts of the case. What is also at issue here, of course, is the difference between doing something wrong by objective standards to which, in a particular case, an individual may not subscribe, and acting wrongly in free acknowledgement of one's moral guilt. In the former case one may experience considerable psychological discomfort through having acted at variance with the views of others whom one respects and whose esteem is valued. And in the latter case this may also be accompanied with feelings of personal guilt or remorse for one's behaviour. But in neither case does it automatically follow that the ensuing consequences of one's action will be invariably and totally harmful, either to oneself or to others. One outstanding instance of this today is the case of those who may have remarried after divorce, and some of whom at least are prepared to brave the disapproval of their fellow-believers and even to tolerate considerable personal misgivings about the rightness of their action, as a price worth paying for the happiness and fulfilment which they now experience, perhaps for the first time. If beliefs, in other words, are to be worthwhile, they are to be valued and esteemed for their own sake and not simply on the grounds of a questionable corollary that the absence of belief is accompanied by an absence of human happiness and wellbeing.

For the believer, then, it would be more consistent and more acceptable to base his objection to the use of donor material not simply on allegedly damaging personal consequences as that which makes such use morally objectionable in principle, but only as confirmation and evidence (when and only to the extent that such is forthcoming) that it is already wrong in itself for other reasons and regardless of consequences, whether good or bad. Such reasons can only be the religious ones of the exclusive covenant relationship which God established between man and woman at creation as the institution of marriage, a divinely ordained relationship which mirrors and in some way partakes of the union between God and his people and, for Christians, of the union between Christ and the Church. It is within that closest of personal unions, lived at various levels and expressed in numerous ways, that new human beings are brought into existence and, the believer may maintain, it is only as the expression of such unions that children may morally be brought into existence in the image of God, as the fruit of his creative love and of the co-creative mutual love of husband and wife.

It could no doubt be argued that to make this moral stipulation on the ground of a firm belief in the God-given nature of marriage and the family is to fall victim to objections similar to those which we considered cogent against the unproven assertion that only as a consequence of marital intercourse expressive of interpersonal love may children be brought into existence. It might also be argued that advances in medical science have the function of pressing upon beliefs and of refining their content of all purely human components resulting from ignorance, presumptions and familiar habits of thought. And belief must pay science the courtesy of taking such counter-arguments seriously without too readily or too quickly seeking refuge in mystery. It may be that underlying the circumstantial stress on marriage and the family, which is characteristic of Christian teaching, is the fundamental conviction, with which many more than Christians would agree, that human life is a gift whose transmission should be motivated by love and whose flourishing requires an environment of love. To claim that only between married couples and only within the close community of the family can such creative and nurturing love be found is not, of course, to assert that every marriage and every family will satisfy these requirements. And as an absolute and exclusive factual claim it clearly goes beyond the evidence of various situations which disprove it. What it may be held to urge, however, is that, for all the weaknesses and faults of the institutions of marriage and the family as they exist today, they do continue to provide the most favourable circumstances for the loving transmission and nurturing of human life.

Such theological and social considerations on the introduction of a third party as a solution to marital infertility can also throw light on other applications for which *in-vitro* fertilisation and donor insemination are being considered, or to which they are already being directed, as well as on an argument frequently advanced in support of these applications. The argument is that every woman has an absolute right to have a child, should she so wish; and the conclusions drawn are that this would justify the use of *in-vitro* fertilisation or donor insemination to give a child to an unmarried woman or to a lesbian couple. It is clear that the implications of belief about marriage and the family which we have explored would militate against such applications of modern medical science. And it appears also that to argue against these applications from foreseen harmful consequences is to occupy considerably firmer empirical ground than in the case of donor contribution to an infertile marriage. One of the growing social phenomena causing increasing concern to various bodies in society, including the Churches, is that of the one-parent family, which is not only socially disadvantaged in many ways but in which, it seems fair to say, there is also psychological and emotional disadvantage, particularly for the child. It appears to be the case that children are in danger of being emotionally and sexually (in a broad sense) deprived, or perhaps even harmed, in their upbringing if both a father and a mother are not at hand to cooperate in that delicate and demanding task. No doubt there are, of course, individual instances where such dangers are met with considerable success or perhaps with qualified success, but this does not appear to affect the conclusion that deliberately to set about creating one-parent families is a line of action which will not be in the best interests of the child in such families.

Concentrating attention on the interests and future rights of the offspring is also salutary in considering questions surrounding proposals to enable lesbian couples to have a child, whether by adoption or at the much earlier stage of fertilisation. In such cases there is the particular factor that one can predict with a fair measure of certainty what kind of environment and what positive, if not approving, attitude to homosexual behaviour will influence the upbringing and education of the child. And one would be justified, should such influences be considered undesirable, in concluding with even more force that to bring a child into existence in such conditions would inevitably result in a serious infringement of its natural rights.

In any consideration, then, of the basic argument which underlies the advocacy of these applications of *in-vitro* fertilisation and artificial donor insemination, that it is every woman's right to have a child, should she so wish, it appears that one major qualification must be in terms of the rights of such a child once it is brought into existence. It would, of course, be nonsense to argue that a child could have a right not to be brought into existence, that is, not even to be conceived, but it can be strongly argued that if a child will be born into circumstances which will be seriously harmful or detrimental to it, then there is a moral obligation not to initiate that process. If a married woman, for instance, has a medical history which makes it highly probable that, should she conceive, she will produce a severely handicapped child, then, far from claiming that she has a right to have such a child, one would have to conclude that, on the contrary, she has an obligation not to conceive and produce such a child. Similarly, the growing acknowledgement in Roman Catholic teaching that there can be cases when a married couple decide they would be justified in not having a child, and therefore in having recourse to the infertile period in their marital relations, includes the implication that in some circumstances the right of a woman not to be fertilised arises not only from a right that her life not be endangered or that the interests of the existing family not be seriously harmed on economic or other grounds, but also from a present obligation not to submit a future child to an existence which will impair its human flourishing and development. In other words, to urge as a principle without qualification that every woman has a right to have a child is to advocate a principle of self-fulfilment to the exclusion of other moral considerations, and to incur the danger of viewing such a child not as an end, but rather as a means to an end. And to these considerations arising from the infringement of human rights belief would also add that it is only, but not infallibly, within the covenant of the heterosexual union of marriage that such rights of the person can be respected as the embodiment of interpersonal and lifegiving love, which is the image in marriage of the interpersonal divine reality which we point to when we speak of the Trinity of Persons in God.

What the procedure of *in-vitro* fertilisation has raised as a fundamental and urgent question is the connection between procreation and parenthood. The new possibility of separating genetic parenthood from social parenthood, and of separating both from physiological parenthood, as in the case of host-mothers or womb-leasing, an agreement to carry a child of another woman and to return it at birth, raises questions for society of the utmost gravity and importance, and questions for religious belief which are no less urgent. One temptation for belief is to identify new questions as really old questions in new guise and as a reaction to advance once again old answers. Earlier in this chapter we have seen one instance of this in the moral verdict delivered on the procedure for providing human semen, and perhaps this should alert belief to such a general tendency to consider that there is nothing new under the sun. Another instance arose from the development of transplant surgery and the desirability of living kidney donors, when the Roman Catholic tradition reached for the 'principle of totality', which had been enunciated to condemn punitive or contraceptive sterilisation as a mutilation of bodily integrity which might be justified only if it served the interests of the organism as a whole. The result was to condemn organ-donation as a similar mutilation, without considering that such a term is a wholly inadequate description of the surgical exchange achieved by transplantation and that it leaves entirely out of account the generosity of which such a gift is the expression. It may equally be that developments in *in-vitro* fertilisation, which are having the effect of identifying different types or stages of parenthood, which has hitherto on the whole been a simple concept, will force belief to acknowledge and evaluate individually such elements of parenthood against the background of human love and generosity which it considers morally indispensable to the production and nurturing of new human beings. So, for instance, for all the justifiable concern about financial abuses surrounding recourse to host-mothers acting as a physiological parent to bring to term the child of a marriage which might not otherwise be possible, and for all the undoubted emotional strains involved in such an agreement, the practice itself, as a matter of principle, does not necessarily appear morally improper. Were an artificial placenta or an artificial womb to be devised, the case for its desirability in certain circumstances could be morally justified, and indeed incubators for children born or delivered prematurely already constitute a rudimentary form of an artificial womb. The use of such a resource in circumstances where, for whatever reason, a woman's womb was unable to function properly and safely would be similar to the generally accepted and morally routine recourse to kidney or to heart-lung machines to supply for a failure of other bodily functions. Moreover, recourse to a living and related source of organ donation as highly desirable in some cases of renal failure provides a further parallel to considering the morality of host-mothering. If organ donation can be morally justified, then function donation can be morally justified, with this significant difference that even those who might traditionally object that kidney donation was an unwarranted mutilation which does not serve the interests of the whole organism, and which is irreparable, could not advance the same objection against providing the services only of a bodily function, and only for so long as they were required.

With the human element, of course, psychological and emotional factors are introduced which require careful scrutiny. But psychological and emotional traumas may not be gratuitously prophesied, and it is not difficult to envisage circumstances, perhaps as rare as those indicating the need for live kidney donation, in which the inability of a wife to carry the child of her and her husband might be compensated by the generous offer of physiological motherhood on the part of a sister.

Parenthood shared in this way is a novel concept, for belief as well as for society, but novelty is not an invariable indication of moral wrongness. And the same may be said of the new-found ability arising from *in-vitro* fertilisation techniques to space out parenthood, not just between pregnancies but also within the course of one pregnancy. The freezing and banking of human semen, and proposals to freeze and bank human embryos, are enterprises which shock many people, and yet when they are looked at carefully and within the context of the family, it does not appear that their use must be absolutely condemned on moral grounds. There are, of course, many considerations arising from experimentation and from risks of failure or genetic deformity, and these we shall examine in our fourth chapter. Given, however, that such reservations can be met, there appears no inherent objection on moral grounds to a process of what could be called delayed, or suspended, parenthood in families where particular circumstances might favour it. Short-term freezing and holding of husband semen might be indicated until all the other conditions are present for artificial insemination by the husband. And such treatment of semen may also be desired if a husband's health is such that it may in course of time lead to sterility or castration at a stage when he and his wife would wish to increase their family. Freezing and banking human embryos, and thus introducing a pause between genetic and physiological parenthood, clearly has for some people many much more serious implications, including fundamental questions about the beginning of human life and, particularly for the believer, about the existence of the human soul and its direct creation by God. Granted, however, that such questions can be satisfactorily answered, then such treatment of human embryos in the short term might be a necessary part of waiting for the woman to receive the embryo in the most favourable conditions, or of using healthy semen rather than possibly endangering it by freezing it. And in the long term other considerations might arise, such as the fact that ova in particular can begin to deteriorate genetically during the reproductive span of life, to result in disorders such as mongolism, or Down's syndrome, in a future child. For various reasons, then, and not least the desire to produce a healthy child of a marriage, fertilisation and production of an embryo early, or at a particular stage, in a marriage might appear desirable with the purpose of resuming the process of active parenthood in due and appropriate time. Nor does it appear that such an adoption of prolonged parenthood is necessarily in itself morally objectionable.

If the fundamental question central to all these considerations on the application of *in-vitro* fertilisation techniques is the connection between procreation and responsible parenthood, then another equally basic issue which calls for close scrutiny is the connection between the exercise of human sexuality and procreation. Earlier in this chapter we have argued that recourse to artificial insemination and *in-vitro* fertilisation are in principle morally acceptable using only the contributions of husband and wife, since their actions can be seen as motivated by, and expressive of, their mutual love and their shared desire for a child as the fruit and the culmination of their union. The major thrust of Pope Pius XII's argument against the use of these techniques even within marriage was that they are a method of producing a child who is not the result of a loving interpersonal union, or, in other words, that procreation which is contrived without love is morally unacceptable.

It is of interest to note that when, in 1968, Pope Paul VI reiterated his Church's traditional moral rejection of contraception, he appeared to take up this line of argument of his predecessor and convert it into a fresh argument against contraception.

> Men rightly point out that imposing the use of marriage on one's partner without regard to the partner's condition or just wishes is not a true act of love and is to that extent opposed to that concern for each other's interests which the moral order requires. Equally they should admit on consideration that an act of mutual love which impairs the faculty of procreating life which God the Creator of all has built into it according to specific laws, is counter both to the divine plan for instituting marriage and to the will of the primary Author of human life.[3]

In other words, if it is true that procreation which is not the result of mutual love-making is morally wrong, then it is equally true that mutual love-making which actively hinders procreation is morally wrong.

Of the other arguments which Pope Paul marshalled against contraception some were negative in nature, others positively analysed the action itself to judge it inherently bad, and yet others pointed to the harmful consequences which would result from approving the practice. The central argument, however, apart from the constant tradition of the Roman Catholic Church's teaching, was that within the act of marital intercourse there is both a unitive and a procreative aspect, and that God has established between these aspects an indissoluble bond which man may not put asunder. It is a matter of history that the force of this and Pope Paul's other arguments against contraception has not been universally accepted, even among members of his Church. This fact was noted by several of the bishops who spoke at the Synod held in Rome in 1980 on the subject of Marriage and the Family and who asked for more successful reasons to be sought in support of their Church's teaching. It was also adverted to by Pope John Paul II in the following year, in his Apostolic Exhortation which summed up and reflected upon that Synod, and it led the Pope to invite theologians 'to provide enlightenment and a deeper understanding' of Church teaching in this area.[4]

There can be little doubt, then, that for many concerned in the Roman Catholic Church, the present situation with regard to contraception, or what we earlier termed negative fertility control, is highly unsatisfactory. In the absence of truly and universally cogent arguments a problem for many, and particularly for married couples, is that their religious faith is being subjected to very considerable strain. The moral condemnation of contraception is not proposed as a revealed dogma of the Christian religion, nor indeed is it propounded infallibly as being absolutely incontrovertible. It is a teaching which appeals both to papal authority and to reason, and which is argued at considerable length as depending both on the force of rational argument and on the authority of the Church's mandate to teach moral doctrine. If individuals find themselves unable to understand or to accept the force of the rational arguments proposed, then the twofold basis for accepting the teaching is undermined, and they are compelled to put the full weight of their acceptance on simple acceptance in faith of their Church's teaching authority, or *magisterium*, in this area of human and Christian behaviour. It cannot be matter for surprise if not everyone's belief in the Church's teaching authority can take the strain in this area and accept on faith what is not, strictly speaking, a matter of faith, with the unfortunate result that faith in Church teaching on other moral matters may also be weakened and religious belief in the Church itself be shaken. If, then, the community of the Church is to make progress in discerning further the Creator's will concerning the sexual expression of married love and its connection with procreation, a question which acquired new urgency through the medical development of the anovulant pill, this issue is clearly one which extends far beyond routine negative fertility control to engage the Church in careful scrutiny of the function of procreation and the inmost nature of interpersonal married love. When Pope Pius XII urged the indissolubility between intercourse and procreation, in the 1950s, with the former as a morally indispensable precondition for procreation, he was teaching within the centuries-old tradition which allotted in marriage a primacy to procreation over other secondary 'ends' of marriage, a hierarchy of ends which was publicly and definitively abandoned ten years later by the Second Vatican Council and which has vanished from the Roman Catholic Church's Code of Canon Law in its most recent 1983 edition. It may be that so historic a shift in perspective has not yet had time to be assimilated with all its implications into Roman Catholic thinking. And if it is now acknowledged, with further reflection on the stages by which artificial insemination by the husband and *in-vitro* fertilisation may be morally undertaken, as we have argued, that the idea of procreation is now rendered by medical advance an increasingly complex concept which morally need not always be linked inseparably with marital intercourse, then possibly this explication of procreation may in time throw further light on the nature and function of intercourse within marriage.

It is clear that both procreation and intercourse are not simply biological events but also human events to be evaluated morally in the light of their capacity to express and be 'carriers' of human love. It seems equally clear that not only pro-creation, but also contraception, call for careful analysis as terms ascribed to human behaviour and morally evaluated. Thus, for instance, the moral condemnation of 'contraceptive intercourse' as 'frustrating' deliberately the procreative poten-tial of loving physical union would not apply in the case of a wife for whom the anovulant pill had been prescribed as medi-cal treatment for some gynaecological disorder. Nor would it apply in cases where sexual intercourse was forced upon a woman against her legitimate wishes, and where, in fact, she would be morally justified in taking measures, whether before, during or immediately after the event, to ensure that concep-tion did not ensue from such an assault. In such instances, even were she unable to resist being compelled to submit, she would still be entitled to ensure that the full force of the assault could be protected against. Again, increased recognition of the various stages of procreation which has resulted from the development of *in-vitro* fertilisation and subsequent reimplan-tation of the fertilised ovum enables us to distinguish more clearly between the capacity to conceive and the capacity to conceive and carry a child to successful delivery, which is globally referred to as the capacity to procreate. The fact that a woman is able to conceive does not necessarily mean that she is able to procreate, as histories of repeated miscarriage can abundantly testify. In such cases, where the process of pro-creation, once initiated at conception, would be inevitably doomed to failure, it does not appear that the moral condemna-tion of contraception on the grounds of excluding procreation from loving intercourse is relevant. It could be concluded, then, that a woman who may be able to conceive, but unable to procreate in the full and normal meaning of the term, would be morally entitled to take steps to ensure that she would not conceive as a consequence of marital intercourse. And this analysis could proceed further by more and more careful examination of what is meant by describing a series of human events as 'procreation'. The case just considered applies to a woman who cannot deliver a live child, but consideration might also be given as to whether production of a severely handicapped child might, in any normal use of the term, be described without qualification as the capacity to procreate, and whether the safe production of a child which gravely endangered the health of a pregnant woman, not to mention entailing her death in or after the process, could simply be described as indicating her capacity to procreate as that term is generally understood.

That much at least can be said of what we have termed negative control of human fertilisation. If we now return to the more dramatic possibilities offered to society for positive control, it is worth stressing that in our consideration of these we have carefully referred to *in-vitro* fertilisation as being in principle morally acceptable within marriage and only within marriage, and it is important to clarify the phrase 'in principle'. Some of the procedures resorted to as part of the development of *in-vitro* fertilisation and as part of its application do not appear to be essential to the technique and also give cause for grave moral disquiet. This concerns not only the possible destruction or abortion of embryos or fetuses which may develop abnormally, but also the practice of multiple fertilisations. In some cases two, or more, fertilised ova are reimplanted, and this may be compared with the natural conception of twins or triplets, should all successfully develop. In such instances there is the positive intention and hope that at least one will survive. But in other cases, where the fertilised ova are not reimplanted, but are abandoned in favour of a better specimen or are deliberately created for experimentation or as a control for a reimplanted ovum, fundamental issues are at stake about the origins of human life and about its moral status which are of profound concern to society and to religious belief. These we shall consider in our third chapter, observing only for the present that some truths and some scientific advances can be morally tainted by the methods by which they have been acquired, whether they be truths about animal and human tolerance to pain, about human sexual behaviour, or about the development of the human embryo. The dilemma for many people is that such truths and techniques once acquired become part of the common treasury of human knowledge and that it would be senseless to decline to benefit from such knowledge if its use could reduce human suffering and misery. And yet, were the only means of acquiring such knowledge means which are morally repulsive, such people would wish to observe *non tali auxilio*, and prefer that the knowledge had not been sought.

Another major cause for moral disquiet about the many possible applications of *in-vitro* fertilisation arises from its possible exploitation for financial reward. It is no doubt possible to sensationalise here unduly, and the idea of 'trafficking' in human embryos may appear to the medical profession in general to be an unduly emotional one. And yet, as what begins as a most laudable and desirable technique and means of solving infertility problems for individuals acquires a social dimension, and as its numerous other applications come to be explored, it is inevitable that the financial implications of providing such services will also arise. No doubt social climates vary as to how acceptable financial return is considered for the provision of medical facilities and resources. In Britain, for instance, as distinct from some other countries, there is an honoured practice of voluntary blood donation, and many would find it thoroughly distasteful to expect to be paid for helping another in his need for blood transfusions. Even in Britain, however, semen donors can receive a fee for their contribution to the artificial insemination service, and doubtless such a transaction is seen as no more reprehensible than any other in which an individual may legitimately expect to make a profit for the provision of a service to those who need it. A similar mentality can operate with the supplying of female ova, or, along the lines publicised recently by the press, with receiving payment considerably more than incurred as expenses in return for bearing a child for another woman, whether by being inseminated artificially by her husband or by acting as host-mother. The marketing of human embryos to infertile couples, or to single women, is not an outlandish possibility in societies which have already seen 'baby-farming'.

All sale, of course, involves a corresponding need or desire, whether genuinely experienced or artificially stimulated, and evidently some individuals have no moral qualms about selling semen, ova or embryos, so long as customers are to be found for such commodities. Herein, of course, lies the crux, whether semen, ova and embryos can be considered simply as marketable commodities, or whether there is about such human products a particular quality which renders it morally inappropriate that they be so dehumanised. Popular emotional reactions are not moral barometers, and yet they may at times be straws in the wind. And it may have been morally significant when several years ago news that aborted and dead fetuses were not only being used as material for medical experimentation but that they were actually being sold for this purpose was met with widespread public revulsion, to such an extent that it led to a Government enquiry. At the very least, the sale of human embryos for profit, whatever might be said of semen or ova, is a matter which society cannot afford to ignore, and this will be considerably more the case as increased moral status is accorded them, regardless of whether they are to be purchased for implantation or for observation and experimentation.

When one considers the manifold implications and various applications of this revolutionary turning-point which *in-vitro* fertilisation has placed before society it appears manifestly clear that society must be in a position to scrutinise and control them. In our final chapter we shall be considering the moral controls which medical science may be expected to exercise upon itself in the fields of research and experimentation, and indeed what social controls may also be required in those fields. Once, however, science has presented society with its perfected innovation, that innovation becomes the property of society, and the responsibility for how it is to be applied devolves upon society. In the case of *in-vitro* fertilisation, what is at stake is not simply the fate of hitherto infertile marriages, but the quality of life for society as a whole, the future of interpersonal relationships, the institutions of marriage and the family, and the human rights of individuals. Nothing short of parliamentary legislation and international agreements can protect these essentials of society and dispassionately monitor the steps which society may wish carefully to take into its biological and human future.

One consideration which appears to call for legal clarification is the status in law of the human embryo. Societies which legislate to enable abortion will clearly be unwilling to accord fully human legal status to the fertilised ovum. And yet by any standards it is something possessed of remarkable human potential. Who owns it? And may not legal conditions be laid down for the transfer of ownership and the uses to which it may be put? It is apparently the case that the ownership of a corpse is a legal anomaly. If prevention of a similar anomaly could be achieved in the case of the human embryo, then perhaps legislation concerning the rights and limits of such ownership would be the best means of exercising control over the uses to which the human embryo is subjected. The statement by the Medical Research Council on research related to human fertilisation and embryology, which we shall consider in more detail later, refers to the need for 'informed consent' from donors of sperm and ova as a condition of engaging in research on them, and this applies not only to research on sperm and ova individually, but also to ova fertilised *in-vitro*.[5] There is here a rudimentary acknowledgement that some factors call for recognition in the disposition and fate of such genetic material, and this acknowledgement is something upon which social controls may be built. What is not acknowledged is that there is an appreciable difference, even in biological terms, between sperm and ovum on the one hand, and a fertilised ovum on the other, such that donor consent, even mutual, in the latter case should be regarded as not simply exonerating the researcher from any consequences of his research, but also as something itself subject to certain restrictions and controls.

A similar absence of discrimination is evident in the report of the Ethics Committee of the Royal College of Obstetricians and Gynaecologists, in its section giving detailed consideration to legal aspects of artificial insemination and *in-vitro* fertilisation. What may be welcomed is the Committee's finding that

33

there is need for legal registration and licensing in this 'highly sensitive area where human life is being created under artificial circumstances and where there is scope for commercial exploitation of those who are longing for a child'.[6] What, on the other hand, appears strange is that, on the grounds that the problem 'is strictly an ethical one', the Committee sees no place for legal control of embryonic research or experimentation. Nevertheless, it does consider that 'frozen embryos remain the property of the parents', and advises that 'when sperm, ova or embryos are donated the donor should surrender all rights to interest or ownership'.[7] And from this recognition that ownership and property rights, especially relating to the human embryo, do have to be taken into account it appears both practicable and desirable for society to legislate with an eye to the interests of the embryo.

We have argued, then, that with the advent of *in-vitro* fertilisation a revolutionary turning-point has been reached by society which raises issues far beyond solutions to individual infertility. We have identified the ways in which belief, reflecting on this major advance, may welcome it warmly in its application to fill the void of childlessness within many families, and to enable wives and husbands to express in new ways an effective love for each other while accepting into their embrace the ultimate physical expression of their love. We have expressed reservations, based not simply on the projection of unhappy consequences, but on the nature of marriage and family as understood by belief, about the introduction of donor material to alleviate the symptoms, or some of them, of infertile marriages. And, with perhaps more empirical confidence, we have expressed serious moral misgivings about the use of positive fertilisation procedures outside marriage. Finally, we have argued the need for social control over the application of these new procedures, not simply by discipline within the science itself but by legislation which will include some protection of the interests of the human embryo.

At the beginning of this chapter we compared *in-vitro* fertilisation with the development earlier this century to harness the enormous potential of nuclear power. In this development of medical science mankind has been given the power to manipulate human life at its origin, with implications for society's future life, and the quality of that life, which, it does not seem exaggerated to say, could be no less portentous than the nuclear power now at man's disposal. In later chapters we shall be engaging religious belief and bio-ethics in further dialogue concerning the very beginning of human life, and medical research and experimentation. In all of these issues, including the subject of this chapter, the search for truth and human wellbeing inevitably raises fundamental questions concerning purpose. And there appears no better central vantage point in medical care from which to survey such fundamental questions, as well as a host of other more tactical questions, than the stage of human living which we know as dying and death, which will be the subject of our next chapter.

Death and Dying

From time to time it falls to most of us to learn of the death of a relative, friend or colleague, and to experience the fact that death cuts life down to size and imposes a sense of priorities on our living. The sad and sometimes shocking news of a friend's death can often stop us in our tracks, and brings with it a desire and a sense of duty to drop everything, if humanly possible, and to be present at the funeral service to pay our last respects and expressions of human farewell as well as to comfort the bereaved and each other in our sad loss. For the believer, all this will be permeated with the religious urge to pray for their eternal rest and happiness with God, and to console each other with the sure and certain hope of the resurrection. Time is taken from work, meetings and other engagements are postponed or re-arranged, travel arrangements are made, and in all a sobering sense of proportion is laid upon the daily activities of life. For a time, the simple fact and the sheer inevitability of death are recognised and acknowledged for what they are, the abiding backcloth against which we act out our lives.

What medicine has done, and continues to do, is to question that sheer inevitability of death and dying. In unremitting pursuit of human wellbeing in the face of disease, disaster and dissolution, medicine is committed to life rather than death, to vital function rather than dysfunction and, when all else fails, to comfort rather than discomfort. This profession of medicine is, in human terms, a most honourable one. And in religious and Christian terms it is even more than that. From the standpoint of belief, it is a calling to share in the healing ministry of Christ Jesus, who came among us to cure man's bodily as well as his spiritual ills, and who voluntarily took death upon himself in order to confront it, and to cut death in its turn down to size by vindicating the ultimate supremacy of life with God.

What medicine does, as does every attempt at human betterment in other fields such as social justice and work for peace, is
to communicate even now in human society the life-giving
power of the risen Christ, and to share, in however partial and
temporary a manner, in his victory of ultimate liberation from
disease and death.

At the same time, by its various advances and the techniques
and refinements which it offers to society, medical science
poses for mankind and to belief questions of considerable
perplexity which have to do with intermediate choices relating
to the improvement of human wellbeing, and also with long-
range and fundamental choices relating to human destiny. One
such, with which it may be illuminating to approach these
questions is the subject of brain death. Discussion of this
subject appears to have died down, at least in the mass media;
although it is worth noting that very recently, as a result of
controversy about two years ago, the Department of Health
has issued precautionary guidelines for the diagnosis of brain
death and for the circumstances in which this should be undertaken, including complete dissociation from medical personnel
involved in procedures of organ transplantation.[1] It was in this
context of cadaveric kidney and heart transplantation that in
Britain the subject of brain death aroused public attention, and
disquiet, when it was first mooted some years ago. For many of
the general public it was a startling idea that the centuries-old
criteria of heart and pulse beat and of respiration, universally
recognised and commonly recognisable, should now appear to
be discounted in favour of a much more refined criterion
discernible only to an élite of highly trained experts. The alarm
of some interested non-medical, and even medical, parties was
increased at the time by the apparent possibility that the new
definition of death was a definition with a vested interest, since
brain death was publicly advocated in a report of the British
Transplantation Society as a definition it was 'necessary' to
accept in order to ensure a more adequate supply of undam-
aged cadaveric organs, particularly kidneys for transplantation into patients with renal failure. This juxtaposition of brain
death with the speedy removal of vital organs could give the
impression of offering a new Procrustean definition of death,
adjusted to the needs of others, as the author wrote in *The*

Times in reaction to the report of the British Transplantation Society.[2]

The concern expressed was not at the discounting of respiration and heart-beat which were being sustained artificially, so that one was in effect simulating life in a corpse. It was expressed at what was understood to be the fact that, in the absence of cerebral activity, one might discount even spontaneous heart-beat which could survive at least for a short period after sustaining machines had been switched off. In such cases it was envisaged that a beating heart might be removed in good condition for transplantation, and it was also claimed that such a heart might, or even ethically should, be removed while the patient was still on the machine, without switching off to discover whether spontaneous heart-beat might continue. The question raised by the author, whether one would bury a patient whose heart was still beating, may well have appeared unenlightened and unhelpfully emotional to medical experts, but it was not intended to reject, but only to probe, the new definition of death, particularly at a period when its implications were being absorbed by coroners' and criminal courts, and when there were even alarming reports of mistaken diagnosis and of one American patient diagnosed as brain dead who recovered on his way to the mortuary.

Now, however, the idea and the criterion of brain death appear to be universally accepted with more equanimity. If nothing else, the public debate may be seen as illustrating the important truth, not only in medicine but also in other areas, including religious belief and theology, that new ideas require time to be generally assimilated even by experts, but particularly by non-experts. They can call for considerable readjustment and adaptation of one's system of thought, a rearrangement of one's mental furniture to accommodate the introduction of a new piece and perhaps calling for the abandonment of an older and cherished piece. And this introduction of new ideas in society calls for sensitive and understanding realisation of the mental shock, both present and 'future', which they can bring with them until they are slowly assimilated, perhaps simply in their own right and perhaps by comparisons or analogies with other areas of experience. Thus, the idea of brain death as death of the human individual may be usefully compared with the 'run-on' which can sometimes occur to the engine of a car after the ignition has been turned off. Both appear to come to the same thing, residual power or energy working its way out of the system even though the source of the energy no longer exists.

Perhaps one other reflection on the subject of substituting death of the brain for more traditional criteria in determining death of the human person, namely, that the debate is between criteria advanced in each case by medical science, is important to stress. For ultimately it is only medicine, and not religion, which identifies the onset of death in ordinary human terms. Belief may have its own explanation of what happens to the individual at death, and has traditionally described this in terms of the human soul leaving the body. The difficulties of such terminology and such description we shall consider in the next chapter, but for the present it is sufficient to state that the awesome responsibility of actually identifying the moment of death belongs only to medical science. As Pope Pius XII observed in 1957, human life continues for as long as its vital functions, as distinct from the simple biological life of the organs, manifest themselves spontaneously or with the aid of artificial processes, and the task of determining the exact instant of death is that of the physician.[3] We may conclude, then, that in this area society can, and should, do no other than place its trust in the medical profession and the medical practitioner, but that in a matter of what may understandably be considered vital interest it should be an alert trust, conscious of human fallibility and of the many pressures to which the practice of medicine is subject in its pursuit of human and social betterment and of the best for the patient.

The concern to do what one may consider best for one's patient leads to another issue connected with the process of dying, that of euthanasia. As a final resort for individual medicine, and as a social programme, euthanasia is, of course, actively supported by various bodies in society and is regularly proposed as a fit subject for enabling legislation. At its best, advocacy of euthanasia may be seen as focusing a continuing and genuine, if despairing and misleading concern to alleviate the indignities and distress of terminal illness as well as of other conditions. And in considering such a project we are examining what may be termed the ultimate test of determining whether good motives are sufficient to make good morality. To put someone out of his or her misery is quite obviously a praiseworthy concern, unless one is committed to the entirely inhuman, and therefore radically un-Christian, view that pain and suffering are experiences which are desirable in themselves and to be encouraged. The Christian belief is that when suffering is unavoidable it can be vested with a positive interpretation and a creative power. But it is also a fact that pain can diminish human living, and can be a crushing and disintegrating experience. For some, the voluntary acceptance of suffering can be a personal vocation, but it is not one to be foisted or forced on others for, as it were, their own spiritual good. And at least some of the motivation behind euthanasia can well be approved by religious belief.

Against the practice itself many types of argument can be marshalled, of which the most obvious is that killing a person as a means of alleviating his or her distress is an unnecessary procedure, since that distress can less drastically be countered by judicious treatment which is either at present available or which could be made more widely available given suitable allocation of resources and suitable training of personnel. Such is the positive philosophy underlying the hospice movement; and a recent report of a working party commissioned by the Linacre Centre and chaired by the writer contains most valuable suggestions and considerations from its medical members of 'positive alternatives to euthanasia, alternatives which as individuals we should want to support and for which as a society we urgently need to provide resources'.[4]

Shortage of such resources, however, whether at a national or a local level, can still leave a difficulty of coping with intractable distress, at least in perhaps isolated instances; and to the advocacy of euthanasia in such instances another line of argument is opposed, that of the widespread consequences which would follow from countenancing such a practice, and to what, even unintentional, abuses it might be subject. It is here that the distinction between voluntary and involuntary euthanasia is most hotly debated, 'voluntary' being that which is requested by a person, either at the time or in anticipation, and 'involuntary' being that administered to a patient who may be unable, through age or lack of awareness, to request it or even wish it. Once grant the practice of voluntary euthanasia, it is charged, and the dividing line will inevitably and readily be crossed to 'involuntary'. For if euthanasia is a benefit to a patient, why should it be limited only to those capable of requesting it? To this line of arguing from consequences others are added affecting the genuine freedom of a request for euthanasia in the light of pressures about being a burden upon others or even being in some sense expected to request it; or in considering whether the request itself is an entirely rational one and not the expression of a transitory depression, which might, moreover, leave no room or time for change, or for an improvement or alleviation of the condition. And once granted the possibility of involuntary euthanasia, then the pressures on the person to administer it could make the freedom of the decision equally suspect or the motivation subject to moral questioning.

The whole questioning of the administering of death, when seen in these terms of possible errors, abuses and other likely consequences, is a most formidable one, and one which leads many to conclude that the dignity and the value of life in general, and the good of society, require a strong bulwark of moral and legal prohibition of such a practice. But, it could be argued, abuses can be controlled, and undesirable consequences can be countered, although attempts at framing legislation have invariably found it well-nigh impossible to close off all undesirable practices and loopholes. To this the answer of religious belief would be to direct attention to much deeper considerations, and focus it upon not the suffering and distress, but on the person experiencing it. Faith would urge that, even upon purely human considerations, there is an element of sheer mystery about human existence which lays a claim upon men to reverence and respect it, to foster it and not to destroy it. Even on the most ordinary grounds, and apart from any religious considerations, human life is a deep mystery. None of us can give a complete account of ourselves, far less of each other. We can in some measure account for our origin, we can strive to make some sense of our existence, and we can conjecture about our future. But at the heart of each one of us is an intractable, perhaps impenetrable, personal core. And at the heart of human society, which originates in a multitude of such personal beings, and is ordained to their individual and collective wellbeing, lies this basic mystery of the sheer given-ness of human living and human existence. It is that which is the subject matter of medicine, whose only appropriate fundamental response to it can be one of wonder and reverence.

Christian belief considers this mystery and unfolds it to uncover new depths, finding human living to be rooted in God's life-giving love, which both explains its origin and destiny, and at the same time erects limits around it on which man may not trespass. The traditionally fundamental Christian objection to suicide and euthanasia is that God is master of life and death, and man only the steward to whom his life has been entrusted. God is *dominus*, or owner, and man is *servus*, or servant and underling, who will eventually have to give before God an account of his stewardship of his life. Implicit, or even explicit, in the contract is that man may not relinquish his use of life, or his stewardship of life, just when he so wishes, but only when God, its owner, so decides. There is much truth in this way of describing man's relationship with God, which relies heavily on the steward and talents parables of Jesus in the Gospels. But like all human language it suffers from being inadequate if it claims to exhaust in one type of terminology the whole delicate relationship between man and his God. Specifically, as the language of justice, it can too easily present God as a demanding and unforgiving absentee landlord, ready to pounce on his errant stewards when he returns from having left man to get on with his own life. To talk of a just God, and to think that one has then said everything about his attitude to us, is to encourage an idea of him as remote and aloof from his creatures. But the Christian good news is that God is love; that he is profoundly, even passionately, concerned for each one of us as individuals; and that our life is a gift of his love, to be cherished both for its own sake, and on account of the giver and his intentions for its use and its flourishing during this life and beyond. Far from life being something to be transacted under the vigilant eye of a heavenly Judge, it is a shared enterprise and pilgrimage hand-in-hand with God in Christ. And dying is not, at heart, a lonely struggle in isolation from a distant God whom one longs to join; it is a final stage in that pilgrimage which is surrounded and bathed in God's friend-ship, in which, the Christian believes, as throughout life, he is sustained by God's 'everlasting arms'. Viewed in this context, euthanasia is not an injustice towards the Lord God, but a disappointment of his personal trust and a rejection of his abiding presence.

What, however, of the unbeliever who cannot enjoy such consolations of religion? For such, faith maintains, the active presence and support of the loving God who made him are as much a reality as they are for the believer, whether perceived as such or not, and whether within or mediated through the support and care of those in attendance upon the dying person. For believer and unbeliever alike, the central consideration here is that of companionship in dying, and of the strength and support of human love within which, for the believer, are contained in sacramental fashion the ministrations of God's own love. Whatever else, then, may be urged in more human arguments relating to the utter mystery of human life and the dangerous consequences of admitting euthanasia, it is the mys-terious purpose of God's continually creative love which is the ultimate and foundational argument for the believer opposed to euthanasia. Life is seen as more than a task, and viewed as God's gift, not to be thrown back at him but to be cherished as containing within it the promise of even more abundant life after death in even closer companionship with the God who is love.

An alternative consideration which then arises from viewing life as a gift of God which may not be returned to him prema-turely, and which plays a significant part in arguments favour-ing euthanasia, is whether life should be jealously held on to, or sustained at all costs, when all the signs are that death is imminent or inevitable. In more prosaic terms, as expressed in Clough's well-known couplet, need one 'strive officiously to keep alive'? It is here that there arise questions concerning the use of drugs, intensive care, and the distinction between so-called 'ordinary' and 'extraordinary' means of preserving and sustaining life. Over the years this distinction has proved of some importance and value in providing a moral rule for types of medical treatment, but like all rules it is in danger of be-coming detached from the reflection and thinking which it encapsulates, and even of introducing confusion rather than clarity into the situations with which it attempts to deal. What underlies the statement that normally we are obliged to resort to ordinary means of preserving life but not to extraordinary means? And what do these terms mean in modern medicine? It seems important to realise, first, that the terms are relative, and, second, that they refer not so much to types of treatment as to the effects of such treatment on differing individuals. Underlying the distinction is the attempt to estimate the degree of burden, as distinct from alleviation, which any particular treatment will impose on the patient. And that must vary from patient to patient. To that extent the distinction is about quality of life resulting from the projected treatment.

Once what has been termed 'the process of dying' has been embarked upon, or once past the point of no return (which is a matter of clinical judgement, and not always by any means an easy one), then the delicate balancing of possible treatments has to be undertaken. It is not, of course, a question of choosing whether to treat or not to treat, but of choosing which are the treatments appropriate to the dying person's condition. Clearly, any special treatment which would not improve the condition is uncalled for (as distinct, perhaps, from non-therapeutic experimentation, which we shall consider in a later chapter). Others might arrest the process, or produce some improvement, but at considerable cost to the sick person in terms, for instance, of distressing side-effects, such that, on balance, it would be difficult to consider them an overall improvement of the patient's total state. Some treatments envisaged may prove financially crippling to the patient or his dependents, at least in some countries; others may be taken in their stride by eighteen-year-olds but scarcely by eighty-year-olds; some may have become routine in certain medical centres but accompanied by considerable risks in others; and so on. To all such treatments the term 'extraordinary means' applies, and they are judged extraordinary not by reason of their intrinsic character but because they do not significantly provide a net improvement in the quality of living of the sick person in the context of his life as a whole. Or rather, it would be more accurate to say, a net improvement in the quality of his dying. In effect, the distinction presupposes that a moral judgement has already been taken that not absolutely every attempt need be made to arrest the process of dying once its onset has been identified, and that there is no moral requirement to prolong that process unless the person's state can be significantly, if temporarily, improved. For the purpose of the distinction is to throw light on how the onset of death may be handled and on what is the appropriate treatment for a person in the dying stage of his life.

How this criterion of 'unduly burdensome' is to be applied in specific cases must be a matter both of clinical judgement and of the patient's decision, and on this some further reflections may be appropriate. The first is to advert to the medical truism that one is not treating diseases but patients with diseases, an approach which is confirmed and enhanced by the Christian stress on the dignity of the individual human person. This being the case, there are some ailments, of which perhaps pneumonia is a good example, which in themselves may be remedied today by fairly routine treatment, but whose treatment as contracted by different patients should be considered within the overall personal condition of each patient. It is this aspect of patient, as distinct from sickness, treatment which has gained for pneumonia the name of 'the old man's friend'. Consequently, it might be suggested, if a dying patient were to contract pneumonia, then the decision to treat, not the pneumonia, but the dying person with pneumonia, could well be different from the decision to treat another patient who is not in the process of dying. Pneumonia might be viewed in such a case not as an isolated ailment but as further indication of the general deterioration of the patient's life, which would not be materially improved as a whole by piecemeal medicine.

Some such considerations appear to underlie discussions about routine resuscitation procedures following cardiac arrest. A number of years ago considerable public disquiet arose at the information that general distinctions were being made about classes of patients who were then marked down as 'not to be resuscitated'. In general, however, it appears that the instinctive reaction of hospital personnel is to resuscitate in every case, such is their concern for life. The team-decision relating to individual cases, as to whether or not they should be resuscitated in the event of cardiac arrest is, and should be, based not on the availability and generally presumed desirability of resuscitation for all, but on the prognosis of what such resuscitation would entail for the person affected. May the same be said of much less dramatic treatments of the dying, such as simple nourishment? The answer must, it appears, be in the negative. There may well be cases where ordinary ingestion and retention of food and drink prove impossible or extremely uncomfortable, and in such cases the procedure need not be persisted with, and attention switched to other possible means of nourishment. But nourishment itself, it appears, cannot be classed as medical 'treatment' to be assumed or discontinued, if only because to deprive a person of nourishment is more of the nature of undermining his resources and actively contributing to his death than of simply permitting his illness to take its course. Possibly a comparison with pneumonia may be helpful, in the sense that the fact that pneumonia supervening on an already terminal illness may not necessarily call for vigorous treatment would not justify one in wheeling a dying patient to an open window in order for him to contract pneumonia.

The second reflection on how the criterion of 'unduly burdensome' is to be applied to treatments offered to the dying patient centres on the fact that they are offered, and not simply administered. If degrees of burden vary with individuals, then ultimately only the individual can decide on whether the treatment is worthwhile for him or her. And this introduces a distinction between medicine's offers of various life-sustaining and pain-reducing treatments, which constitute a primary concern of medicine, and the way in which individuals may assess such offers within the context of their whole life and of their personal scale of values. For doctors, professionally, securing health is a very high priority, but individuals may vary in how high in their estimation physical wellbeing is to be placed in their view of life as a whole. A pain-free existence is not automatically to be considered the highest good in the estimation of all, and may often yield to other values and considerations, affecting others, for instance. It is not necessarily a matter of declaring that one crowded hour of glorious life is worth an age without a pain, but of assessing whether the quality of life offered as a consequence of a particular treatment is so diminished for the individual that he, and he alone, would be justified in deciding that he could not accept the burden entailed by the treatment.

This being so, it is clear that the final judgement about the choice of treatment, heavily dependent although it must be on the expertise and experience of medical personnel, must lie with the patient whenever possible, or when this is impossible, with those who know him or her best. Such a conclusion would give moral justification to the developing idea of the 'living will', by which an individual becomes legally entitled to stipulate that, in the event of terminal illness and in the absence of consciousness, he does not wish certain attempts at treatment to be administered to him. It is also a conclusion which gives further moral weight to the principle that a dying person has the right to know the truth about his condition. About this, it appears quite clear, doctors are divided, and many would certainly wish to qualify general subscription to the principle of 'right to know' with therapeutic considerations affecting individual patients, or with the rejoinder that some patients do not wish to exercise such a right and would prefer to remain in ignorance. What does appear to be the case is that any exceptions to the right require justification and that therefore the right is at least generally respected as one possessed by all patients in principle. It becomes important, then, to scrutinise with care any proposed exceptions in practice, and further, how best the patient may be informed about his condition. Protectiveness on the part of the doctor towards his patient is undoubtedly admirable, but, as in so many walks of life, protectiveness can easily slide into paternalism, based on a judgement that the patient does not possess the inner resources or the resilience to accept the tragic information that his life is drawing to a close. And it may well be that the doctor simply underestimates his patient's resources in declining to impart information – which, it must be acknowledged, must be also a painful and time-consuming activity – or even misjudges the patient's real wishes in this matter. In the actual communication, time and timing are of the essence, and it may be necessary to defer it until an appropriate moment. This leads one to conclude that communication which is intended to be truly helpful may require preparation, and that therefore telling the truth is not just a matter of making a truthful statement, but of making such a statement at the right time and in the right circumstances. 'When is truth?' appears to be as relevant a question as 'what is truth?' Nor need such communication of the truth be explicitly verbal, as appeared evident to the author from a recent television discussion on a staged interview between a doctor and an actor playing the role of a victim of unknown cancer. In the studio discussion, which severely criticised the doctor for being vague, contradictory and misleading in his remarks to the patient, no account appeared to be taken of the overall effect of the conversation, of the ebb and flow of individual hints and allusions made by the doctor, building up to a final result of non-verbal communication in which the patient and doctor reached a tacit agreement on the truth of the matter, on which neither was in any doubt.

One major question which arises regularly in connection with any decision to discontinue treatment of a dying patient is the matter of moral responsibility for the death of the patient which ensues. And on this, two comments can be made. The first is that not every decision to allow a patient to die, as distinct from putting him to death, is *ipso facto* morally praiseworthy. Neglect, incompetence of judgement and culpable omission cannot be so easily discounted. The second comment is the more important, and affects the traditional distinction between killing and letting die which is regrettably, because confusingly, described sometimes as merely between two types of euthanasia, active and passive. The polemical, and political, thrust of translating the traditional distinction into types of euthanasia is, of course, to argue that since all agree to passive euthanasia there is little difference in proceeding also to resort to active euthanasia. Such a deliberate blurring of two quite distinct types of action does little for clarity of thought or expression, and ignores the fact that, while on occasion the distinction between allowing to die and killing appears to be a rather thin line, it is nevertheless a firm line. There is a vast difference between, on the one hand, standing back from a dying patient in the resigned realisation that nothing more can be done for him, and on the other hand intervening in his system to put him to death and thus out of his misery. And when it comes to switching off life-sustaining apparatus, there is no moral distinction between, on the one hand, switching off the machine and discontinuing that unsuccessful form of treatment, and on the other hand deciding in the first instance not to put the patient on the machine and initiate treatment. The decisive factor in identifying whether the patient is allowed to die or is killed must be what is identified as 'cause of death'. Perhaps comparison with a runaway car may be illuminating, in considering the efforts of someone to hold it back when it is threatening to crush another to death, but who finally in exhaustion has to let it go. Such exhaustion is certainly a factor in the full sequence of events resulting in the car crushing someone to death, but it cannot accurately be described as 'causing' death or as being morally accountable for the death which ensues.

To discontinue, then, or not to initiate, life-saving procedures which cannot significantly reverse, or even usefully prolong, progressive deterioration of life in the dying cannot be regarded as encompassing the death of a person in this state. The case, however, is far otherwise when the person in question is not in the process of dying, and life-sustaining, as distinct from life-saving, procedures are withdrawn, as occurred in one hotly-disputed instance in England in recent times. The case of *Regina v Arthur*, which resulted in acquittal, centred on the death in hospital of a three-days-old baby suffering from Down's syndrome who had been rejected by his parents and whom the doctor in attendance had instructed to be given 'nursing care only'. Post-mortem evidence indicating brain, lung and heart damage came to light only in the course of the trial and led to an original charge of murder being reduced to one of attempted murder. The acquittal was greeted with delight by some doctors, including a number who had given evidence, as a legal vindication of their own views and practice, but the particular and general issues raised by the case gave many others cause for deep concern about some features of current paediatric practice affecting children born handicapped.[5]

In the course of the trial and of such public debate as was permissible, much reference was made to 'the grey area' in which those treating handicapped babies have to make often very delicate and unenviable decisions. The term appears to be used to identify situations which are neither black nor white but where white shades into black, legal into illegal, ethical into unethical, as indicating a sort of moral no-man's-land in which the individual has no access to moral principles or guidelines, but must simply fend for himself as best he can. A moralist might wish to argue, however, that it is precisely in such 'grey areas' that moral principles and guidelines are most informative and useful, as helping not only to an identification and analysis of such 'borderline' situations, to use another metaphor, but also to a dispelling of mental lack of clarity in approaching and in describing such situations. From the testimony of some paediatricians presented for the defence in the trial in question there is evidence of considerable fog surrounding words and procedures rather than of grey areas of moral dilemmas connected with some practices in neonatal care of the handicapped. Not only do bland formulae such as 'feed on demand' or the prescribing of regular sedatives need to be carefully scrutinised, to assess just why sedatives are prescribed and what kind of 'demand' can be expressed by a sedated child, but, as the rationale which explicitly underlies such forms of treatment, the idea of benignly 'allowing to die' calls for the utmost rigour of moral analysis.

Where medicine would shrink from actively intervening to put a dying person to death, it can find useful clarity and support in distinguishing between such a procedure and other forms of treatment which acknowledge that the process of dying may be, perhaps reluctantly, allowed to run its course. And in such cases 'allowing to die' is a fair description of this surrender on the part of medicine to the inevitability of death. But when what is at issue is not a dying person but a handicapped neonate who is not necessarily dying (and mongolism, for instance, is not a fatal handicap, any more than is in many cases spina bifida), then what can happen is that the ethical and medical principle of 'allowing to die' is torn from its context of someone who is embarked on the process of dying, in which it is formulated as a kind of medical and ethical shorthand summing up that context and the appropriate treatment, and is imposed on an entirely different context, that of a child born handicapped but not dying. And in the process a major ethical shift of perspective occurs, so that the principle which originated from questions about when to let the dying die has now become one of when to let the living die. There is no moral 'grey area' here; there is only fog and obscuration. And it is in the public interest that such fog be dispelled and the reality of some paediatric procedures seen for what they are, on pain of vague and perhaps uneasy public connivance at what can only be described as a policy of euthanasia by deliberate neglect. It is a commonplace that death has replaced sex as the prevailing taboo subject of this century, but medicine does no true service to itself or to society by any appearance of colluding in attempts to ignore unpleasant or distressing features of either death or human handicap. And to such considerations about the simple need for individuals and societies to face human realities, belief would add the further observation that, in his living as in his dying, every human individual is a cherished son or daughter of God, worthy of the deepest respect in his or her own right, not only as embodying the sheer mystery of human existence but also as a unique focus of God's own love and concern with an eventual destiny far surpassing all human imaginings.

3

The Beginning of Life

In the previous chapter, on death and dying, we examined the context within which society may examine the various choices in the management of death which medicine now offers, and we considered how, for the believer, the sheer mystery of existence, on any terms, is offered the key to understanding in life's being seen as the gift of a loving God with its own purpose and destiny. For belief, death is the completion of one phase of our human existence, the closing of one chapter in a personal story which still has exciting and thrilling prospects in store. The purpose of this chapter is to consider the opening of that story and the circumstances in which it begins, with all its promise and potential waiting to unfold and develop in the blossoming of a human life.

If simple human existence is a profound mystery, and the end of our earthly life is also a mystery, how much more mysterious must also be the start of life. The first emergence of *homo sapiens* on this planet is something about which we know almost nothing. Despite the fact that science has advanced various versions of a theory of human evolution, when it approaches the critical stage of qualitative change in what became the human race we are still left with what, for lack of evidence, remains an attractive and impressive theory. Moreover, we appear faced with a fundamental question of what would count as evidence, or be accepted as evidence, to establish the advent of man. Apart from certain physical features, it appears that a critical factor would be evidence of the exercise of rationality. But what such evidence would amount to, it appears, is an indication of the conditions being present for some giant step for mankind to take place, or an indication that it had taken place. It would not tell us what had taken place, or how specifically human life had come into being.

Similar sorts of puzzles surround the beginning of life for an individual member of our species, as to what is happening, how it happens, and when it happens. But there is now the additional dimension that the truths which are being explored are not only important for their own sake, but are also of profound importance for their moral implications, and for the way in which they affect human moral decisions. Within a medical context these are seen today at their most urgent in the debate and controversy surrounding abortion, certain methods of birth-control, and some of the procedures being used or envisaged in the practice of *in-vitro* fertilisation. In considering the question of the beginning of life we are also exploring a moral evaluation of such major human issues.

In 1930, in the papal letter *Casti Connubii* on Christian marriage, Pope Pius XI strongly condemned the practice of abortion even to save the life of the pregnant woman. An argument which he rejected was that, in a case where the presence of a fetus constituted a danger to the life of the mother, it could be considered, in traditional moral terms, as an 'unjust aggressor', or as unjustifiably threatening the life of the mother, and that she would then be morally entitled to defend herself against that attack by repulsing the attacker even if this entailed killing it. The counter-argument which Pius XI raised against this conclusion was to deny that anyone could reasonably consider a tiny innocent child in its normal habitat of the womb as an 'unjust aggressor' with all the conclusions which might follow from that.[1] This strong teaching on abortion was reiterated by succeeding Popes, including Pope Pius XII in his celebrated address to midwives,[2] and remains part of the Catholic Church's total and absolute moral rejection of any form of deliberately induced abortion. Although the moral ban on abortion undertaken to save the life of a pregnant woman is widely recognised to be by far the most testing and difficult application of Roman Catholic teaching in this field, and although it has been claimed that insistence against abortion even in this case has done much to stimulate improvements in antenatal and perinatal care and treatment, so that it is now a comparatively rare dilemma, reference to it by way of intro-duction to this chapter is useful, because it highlights the fact that in the debate and controversy surrounding abortion there are two quite separate arenas. One is that which centres on the moral question whether it is ever morally permissible to take the life of any human person; and this is a question which ranges over the issues of capital punishment, warfare and self-defence in general, as well as abortion, and draws parallels between all of these instances. The other arena is quite distinct, and ranges over issues of brain death and permanently comatose patients, as well as of abortion in the early stages of pregnancy, and *in-vitro* fertilisation; and that arena concentrates not just on a moral principle, but also on a factual question: what is it that constitutes a human person? The answer to this factual question is of critical importance in moral dilemmas surrounding the beginning of life. If, on the one hand, the conceptus is identified as a human person, then moral questions are seen as a balancing of rights between equals, and the basic moral question is clarified as that which asks whether it is ever morally permissible to take the life of this human person. If, on the other hand, the conceptus is identified as not a human person, or not yet a human person, then the moral question arises as to what rights it may possess, since rights are generally considered to be held only by persons, or as to how what other-than-personal rights or claims it may have are to be balanced against the clearly personal rights of others who are undeniably persons.

This, of course, is why so much controversy surrounds the question of the personal, and therefore moral, status of the conceptus. It is a controversy in which feelings and emotions can tend to run high on all sides, often for the most praiseworthy of causes; in which allegations and imputing of motives can only obscure the issue; and in which facts and moral principles can become slogans and counter-slogans, weapons and counter-weapons. And yet it is also a controversy which urgently requires clarity and calmness of thought and language, not simply dogmatic utterances. And perhaps the most ambiguous term in the entire discussion is that of 'person', which can mean very different things to different people. In ordinary usage it is used to identify someone who is rational, is capable of free choices, and is a coherent, continuing and autonomous centre of sensations, experiences, emotions, volitions and actions. In other words, an adult human being. Taking these as typically human and personal characteristics, one can go back in time to consider the child and even the baby, and say it also is a human person because it possesses the capacity for all these activities, and has begun to exercise that capacity in various observable ways. One can then go back to before birth, and observe certain rudimentary developments and activities at various stages of fetal growth, and thus observe these capacities as themselves in process of emerging. For many who are opposed to abortion the claim is then made that from the moment of conception these personal capacities are already present and await only the gradual development of the organism as the necessary condition for their exercise. In other words, the human person exists from the fertilisation of the ovum. For others, however, the idea of person has now moved so far from ordinary usage and become so attenuated and blurred, so distanced from its ordinary understanding, as to be now altogether meaningless, and indeed misleading. The most they are disposed to concede is that what exists from the moment of fertilisation is something which contains the potential to develop into a human person, but which is not yet a person, on any normal understanding of that word. This view would appear to be asserting that the conceptus does not yet manifest the *activities* of a human person, while the former view maintains that, while this may be the case, the conceptus already possesses the *endowments* of a human person, so that rather than speak of a potential human person one should more correctly speak of a human person with potential.

The debate, however, is not clarified by introducing the idea of potential, since its use on both sides simply reflects and extends the previous fundamental positions. Those who would argue that to describe the conceptus as only potentially a human person is to ignore the fact that even the child at birth, and every adult, is still only potentially a human person are using the term 'potential' to mean the capacity to become more of a person, or more fully a person, in terms of charac-teristically personal activities. While, on the other hand, those who claim that this description of a potential human person applies exclusively to the embryo or fetus at an early stage are using the term 'potential' to mean that it is not yet in any real sense a person at all.

Underlying this ambiguity in understanding the terms 'potential' and 'person' are what appear to be two different philosophies, or ways of understanding reality. One, which has become characteristically Anglo-Saxon and is widespread today in more or less sophisticated forms, is an empirical approach to reality which is not prepared to identify as real what is not observable or measurable in some way, and which tends to dismiss, or at least suspect, anything claiming existence which cannot be empirically or scientifically observed and verified. To that extent it concentrates on behaviour and activity, and is not disposed to ascribe existence or reality to much else. It is a type of reductionist philosophy, which produces the idea of a person as something which acts in certain characteristic and identifiable ways. The other philosophical approach, which has its roots in ancient Greek thought and which has for centuries exercised a powerful influence on Christian thinking, would claim to go behind the observable phenomena and activities to identify their sources, the 'natures' of these sources, and the relationships between these natures. In this approach to experience, which may be considered either a richer or an unnecessarily complicated view of reality, what is stressed is being rather than behaving, the agent rather than just its activities, its inherent resources rather than simply the observable exercise of those resources. It concedes that these resources cannot be brought to action unless favourable circumstances and conditions, such as neurological, physiological and environmental factors, are also present. What it will not concede, however, is that just because the physical structure of the human organism is not yet sufficiently developed for the deployment of its innate and inherent resources, or endowments, then one cannot ascribe to it some already present and gradually developing vital force which is basically what constitutes it as a human person, and indeed is the reason why the organism develops precisely as it does.

This more metaphysical view of the human person, deriving largely from the philosopher-scientist Aristotle, finds its strongest expression in Christian speculation and language about the human soul and about the doctrine of the soul's creation by God. As the spiritual principle in man which organises, sustains and activates his physical component, the human soul's exercise of its intrinsic powers of rationality and volition is obviously also limited by the physical resources available to it at any stage of its existence. But the fact that it is not able at certain stages to exercise its powers, the mind and the will, does not mean that it does not at those periods of its existence possess a mind and a will. From the first moment of its creation by God, its 'infusion' into material reality, the soul exists with all its powers. As an embodied soul it constitutes a human person whose embodiment will become increasingly developed and complex to permit the full range of his or her activities. And for believers the abortion debate over the status of the fetus or embryo or fertilised ovum is also a test of the significance, and indeed the truth, of this Christian doctrine of the soul and its infusion by God in the act of creating each individual human person. Within this philosophy and terminology the debate is crystallised in the question at what moment the infusion of the soul, or 'animation' (ensoulment), takes place. And it cannot be a process, or a gradual development, since the human soul has no material component parts, being a simple spiritual substance, which is present either fully or not at all.

In its strongest form the answer to this question of when ensoulment takes place is at the moment of the ovum being fertilised. The moral consequence of this is obviously that any destruction of the fertilised ovum is the destruction of a human embodied soul, or the killing of a human person, be it by the discarding of ova fertilised *in-vitro* or experimentation upon them, or by the action of intra-uterine devices or other contraceptives which prevent the fertilised ovum from implanting in the lining of the womb (if that is how they achieve their effect), or by abortion at any later stage of pregnancy. It is widely held that this position of 'immediate animation', or ensoulment immediately at conception, is the official teaching of the Catholic Church, but it is also recognised that this has not always been the case. The Greek philosophy and biology, notably Aristotle's, which underlay much scholastic thinking in the Middle Ages held in fact to a process of 'mediate animation', or a biological development of the human conceptus through several intermediate stages of growth considered to be first vegetative and then animal until eventually, some forty to ninety days after conception (depending on whether it was male or female), the organism was sufficiently organised and disposed to be the recipient of the specifically human form, the rational soul. In this tradition a key passage was that of Aristotle's *Natural History* in which, with a wealth of observation, he describes animal reproduction, and on man observes:

> In the case of male children the first movement usually occurs on the right-hand side of the womb, and about the fortieth day, but if the child be a female then on the left-hand side and about the ninetieth day... About this period the embryo begins to resolve into distinct parts, it having hitherto consisted of a fleshlike substance without distinction of parts. What is called effluxion is a destruction of the embryo within the first week, while abortion occurs up to the fortieth day; and the greater number of such embryos as perish do so within the space of these forty days. In the case of a male embryo aborted at the fortieth day, if it be placed in cold water it holds together in a sort of membrane, but if it be placed in any other fluid it dissolves and disappears. If the membrane be pulled to bits the embryo is revealed, as big as one of the large kind of ants; and all the limbs are plain to see, including the penis, and the eyes also, which as in other animals are of great size. But the female embryo, if it suffers abortion during the first three months, is as a rule found to be undifferentiated; if however it reach the fourth month it comes to be subdivided and quickly attains further differentiation.[3]

Accepting the authority of Aristotle that 'the conception of the male is not completed until the fortieth day ... and of the female until the ninetieth',[4] the Church's greatest theologian, Thomas Aquinas, explained the process in terms of Aristotelian philosophy as follows:

> Animal generation is not one simple generation, but a series of generations and dissolutions. First there is the form of the seed [i.e., the first stage of conception], secondly the form of the [coagulated] blood, and so on, until generation is complete. And since dissolution and generation involve the discarding and the introduction of a form, the previously imperfect form is discarded, and a more perfect one introduced, until the conceptus possesses a perfect form. Thus, first there is in the seed a vegetative

soul, which is replaced in the process of generation by another which is vegetative and sensitive, and this is succeeded by the introduction of another which is simultaneously vegetative, sensitive and rational.[5]

Such, for Aquinas, are the stages of human generation in all of Adam's descendants, so that 'our flesh is conceived before it is animated', with the sole exception of Jesus, whose flesh was animated at the moment of conception by virtue of his being conceived miraculously in Mary by the power of the Holy Spirit.[6] And such remained the standard view within the Church until the 17th century, fixing on the time of rational ensoulment of the fetus at forty days after conception. A movement unconvinced by Aquinas' arguments advanced ensoulment to the time of conception, and was approved by the papal physician, but resisted by the Church's leading moralist, Alphonsus of Liguori, although it found some support in the growing devotion to the holiness of the Mother of God, most strikingly expressed in belief in her Immaculate Conception, or, as the defined dogma of 1854 expressed it, belief that Mary was preserved from all stain of original sin 'in the first instant of her conception'. The major motivation, however, on the part of Church authorities to adopt the view of immediate ensoulment was alarm at the proliferation of abortion in society and also concern that the theory of delayed ensoulment appeared to offer some justification for early abortions. Advances in medical science during the 19th century appeared to discredit Aristotelian biology, although neo-Thomists such as Cardinal Mercier continued to hold that the human soul is created by God only when it can be infused in a subject which is sufficiently disposed, and some influential theologians, while still opposed to all abortion, continued to support what had by now become the much less common opinion in the Church. The Church's legislation dropped all reference to less severe penalties for abortions performed before the fetus was 'formed', or the fortieth day, and the strong condemnation of abortion contained in the 1930 papal encyclical *Casti Connubii* did not advert to the question of the time of ensoulment. A similar lack of specification is to be found in the teaching of the Second Vatican Council, in 1965, that 'God who is Lord of life has entrusted men with the supreme charge of caring for life in a manner worthy of man, and therefore life is to be protected with the utmost care from conception onwards; abortion and infanticide are abominable crimes'.[7] In the present context it is relevant to note that an earlier draft of this statement, which referred only to 'life in the womb', appeared to disregard the moral status of the fertilised ovum before entering the womb. It was accordingly replaced by reference to the stage of conception. In presenting the final text, however, which was approved, the drafters explained that 'the time of animation is not touched upon'.[8]

The argument advanced in favour of the position of immediate ensoulment is partly negative and partly positive. Notwithstanding the speculative interpretation of Aristotle and Aquinas about a succession of vital 'forms', or a series of principles of organisation and action following upon conception, no stage of embryonic or fetal development appears so significant as to indicate that a major qualitative change takes place, before which the fetus could be identified as not ensouled and after which it is to be considered ensouled. In the absence of such a critical moment, one is left with the conclusion that the fetus must have been animated, as a fully human person, from the beginning of its existence. In this line of argumentation various candidates for the critical qualitative change in the course of fetal development are rejected: nidation, since this merely identifies the stage at which the fetus attaches to the mother's womb as a source of nourishment and development; the moment of 'quickening' (cf. Aristotle, above), since that is only an experience by the mother of greater mobility of the fetus; viability, since such a stage indicates only that the child can survive, with continual support, in a different environment; and delivery and first breath, since, in spite of the creation narrative of the Book of Genesis (2:7) that God 'breathed into his nostrils the breath of life; and man became a living being', delivery denotes only a successful change of environment. Failing all these alternatives, then, the conclusion necessarily pointed to is that no intervening qualitative change has taken place, but only continuous development of the potentialities which the ensouled human person has possessed from the time it was conceived.

To this argument by way of excluding alternatives, a further positive consideration derives from the science of genetics and from the recognition that from the genetic material contributed by mother and father a new and quite unique genetic package results at conception, which contains within it the full genetic blueprint of a new individual of the human species which will, barring accidents, and without further addition, immediately begin to develop all the latent potentialities of a maturing human person without any radical discontinuity in that development.

As so expounded, the case for immediate animation, and for human individuality and personhood being present from conception, is a strong one. And yet it is not without difficulties, as has been increasingly emerging in recent years. A first such difficulty, it is argued, arises from the high percentage, quoted variously from 30 per cent and upwards, of fertilised eggs which do not implant naturally, but are simply lost and eliminated. Such significant loss raises the question whether each fertilised egg which falls into this category can reasonably be considered to be possessed of an immortal human soul. This argument from wastage relies strongly on the scale of the loss, which is not open to question. On the other hand, if it is simply a proof from numbers, then in principle it does not appear very different, if at all, from arguing from the statistics in some countries, or in earlier centuries, of infant or perinatal mortality to the conclusion that the tragically large number of children who die, or have died, at birth could not possibly be all possessed of an immortal soul. And if this is the alleged force of the argument, then it is not in itself, or considered in isolation, a particularly strong one, even although it does have some appeal to the imagination. If, however, against this consideration of natural wastage it is argued that the loss in such cases is due to some genetic defect in the fertilised ovum, and that therefore one might be able to surmise that in such cases ensoulment has not taken place, such a reply could not only appear evasive but could also be seen as an admission that ensoulment is in some sense dependent on the biological structure of the fertilised egg, either in God's foreseeing how it will develop and infusing a soul or not, depending on its genetic normality, or in God's waiting to see how it does develop before deciding whether or not to animate it. In either case, this view of divine activity is highly anthropomorphic, tantamount to regarding God as a chess-player deciding on a particular gambit in reaction to another's moves. And if the idea of God infusing only some souls at conception in the light of his foreknowledge that these conceptus will develop without early mishap is theologically unacceptable, the only alternative in this line of argument is that God does not infuse any soul until the early stage of development has been successfully surpassed in every conceptus, which is to concede the position of delayed animation. Conversely, if it is argued that God simply decides to animate some fertilised ova at conception and not to animate some others, and that these latter are the ones which for some genetic reason do not survive, this rather despairing line of defence is forced to find some vital principle other than the human soul in the short life of the conceptus which is so divinely discarded. And furthermore it raises very acute questions as to what exactly the human soul itself is, as we shall have occasion to consider later.

The second difficulty, and what for many is the most pressing difficulty against the position of ensoulment at conception, arises not from the large number of fertilised ova naturally lost shortly after conception, but from a major development which can occur to the fertilised ova, apparently during the first two weeks of their existence, that of twinning and of recombination. In some instances of conception, for some as yet unknown reason, the multiplying cells of the embryo can divide into two genetically identical embryos which then continue to develop independently of each other to become identical twins. What is less frequent, but apparently well-documented, is that in some cases two embryos can subsequently combine into one, which then proceeds on its genetic journey as if nothing untoward had happened. The question to be asked, however, of the proponents of immediate ensoulment at conception is to explain precisely what has here happened? In the case of twinning it would appear that a fresh soul has been created and infused into a breakaway embryo, whichever of the two that might be, and that, at least in this case, animation has occurred at a stage later than conception. In the case of two developing embryos fusing to become one, the even more formidable question is that, if previously there were two created human souls from the time of conception, or two human persons, what has become of one of them, and, for that matter, what has become of which one of them?

To these phenomena and the uncomfortable questions which they raise for the position of ensoulment at conception it has been counter-argued that such questions and doubts arise only in the cases where embryos divide and combine, and that, even if one were forced to concede delayed animation in such comparatively rare cases, one is not logically justified in generalising from them to every human embryo, including all those which develop quite normally. Moreover, since we do not know why such statistically abnormal complications arise, it might be that there is some connection between the occurrence of such complications and the possibility that in those cases alone the fertilised ovum has not received a human soul at conception. It may be the unknown cause which brings about twinning and recombination in some few cases, but not in others, which is the deciding factor between immediate animation and delayed animation. To this point, that from some unusual cases one cannot extrapolate to every case, whether unusual or usual, there is clearly some logical weight, even if again the move appears evasive and motivated by a desire to cling to immediate ensoulment. But if one attempts to correlate the ensouled or unensouled status of the embryo with the incidence of twinning and combination, one incurs the same difficulties which we have earlier noted in examining this interpretation of the considerable loss of fertilised eggs. And moreover, it appears that there is a significantly important difference in the case of twinning and combination. Not only is this something which can happen to fertilised eggs in some cases. It appears now to be something which, through *in-vitro* fertilisation techniques outside the womb, can be made to happen in some cases, and in principle could be made to happen in every case. It is not, then, a matter of something inherent in some embryos which lends itself to such developments, so that one might postulate a delayed animation in those cases. It appears to be something inherent in all embryos which can so develop given certain circumstances, including deliberate human intervention.

Some Roman Catholic theologians have begun to consider that the time of implantation of the fertilised egg in the lining of the womb should be considered as the critical stage in it existence denoting creation and infusing of the soul by God. appears likely that the argument from the considerable wastag before that time is a contributory factor in this consideration, but the major element of the argument lies in the inherent possibility for twinning and combination which exists at least until the time of nidation. Underlying this approach appears to be the realisation that some biological stability in the organism is essential for its individuality to be firmly established, and that without this stable individuation of the organism one cannot begin to speak of a human individual. It may be noted, however, that such a line of reflection leading to delayed ensoulment does not proceed by identifying a stage in embryonic development at which a critical qualitative change occurs; it proceeds rather by identifying a stage in that development after which twinning and combination will not, or cannot, occur. This being so, the apparent possibility should be borne in mind that even up to some days after implantation twinning and combination can occur in the womb, while outside the womb, *in-vitro*, it appears that deliberately induced division and sub-division of the fertilised egg can in principle continue indefinitely unless and until some fresh factor appears on the scene. What might that fresh factor be? Possibly the beginning of cell-differentiation rather than mere cell-reduplication. In other words, it might be argued that the biological stability which appears to be a pre-condition of ensoulment is not assured against division of the organism, either *in-utero* or *in-vitro*, until it begins not just to multiply, but to diversify and initiate the process leading to the gradual formation of the various bodily organs and parts. Once this new and differentiating movement has begun, it may be inferred, it is possible with considerably more assurance to conclude that what is present is an irrevocably individual biological subject into which, in accordance with the traditional understanding of creation, a spiritual soul is divinely infused.

A third difficulty raised against the view of human ensoulment at conception stems not from the phenomenon of twinning and combination which, we have argued, can be more positively expressed as requiring biological stability as a pre-condition for ensoulment, but from what is seen as the need for the material into which the soul is received to be sufficiently prepared to receive it by having already begun to develop what is most characteristic of the human person, namely, the brain. A parallel is sometimes drawn with the developing acceptance of brain death which we have considered in the previous chapter and which, occurring as it does at one end of the human life-spectrum, may appear to cast light on events which take place at the opposite end, its beginning. If, it is argued, brain death is death of the human person, however much cellular activity may survive it, then similarly the onset of brain life must be life of the human person, however much cellular activity may have preceded it. And this consideration is seen as confirmation of the more general argument that for personal human life to be present there is first need of a characteristically human biological substratum, which can only be the development of the cerebral cortex during the period of about twenty-five to forty days into pregnancy.

This argument of cerebral development as a pre-condition of ensoulment, however, carries its own difficulties, it would appear. It is not clear whether what is required is the first developments of cerebral tissue, or sufficient development of the nervous system for electrical activity in the brain to be identified (at about eight weeks), or the completing of the brain structure by about the twelfth week. In other words, is it the rudimentary beginnings of the brain as characteristically human, or brain activity as characteristically human, which is regarded as a prerequisite? If it is the cerebral activity which is a criterion of personhood being present, then the argument appears in danger of requiring too much. For what is really characteristic of the human person is not cerebral activity as such, but rational activity. And that does not begin to appear until several years after birth, which, as the scholastic philosophers would say, is inconvenient. Moreover, the analogy with brain death as death of the person to conclude that only with brain life does one have life of the person as such, attractive although it is, has this disadvantage that in each case it presumes that the developed brain is present but not active. For the presence or absence of cerebral activity to indicate the presence or absence of the person requires in each case the presence of a brain which is either active or inactive. And only if the fetal brain were fully developed but not producing any electrical discharge might one argue, by analogy with brain death, that the soul had not yet been infused and that a human person was not present. This condition does not obtain, however, in the progressive development of the human embryo, which, far from being in process of dissolution and disintegration at the end of life is in process of cumulative integration and development at the beginning of life. To concentrate, then, simply on electrical activity as such in the brain, rather than on the development of cerebral tissue, however rudimentary, as indicating the first onset of a distinctively human characteristic in the fetus does not appear warranted.

Even to require simply the development of cerebral tissue, however, as the typically human characteristic without which one cannot yet predicate human personhood of the developing organism, or as the disposition necessarily required for infusion of the rational soul to take place, appears to incur the risk of disregarding the findings of genetics. For it can be argued that the characteristically human biological substratum which the infusion of the soul requires is none other than the human conceptus itself, composed as this is of cells which are genetically human through and through, and which in its turn requires, as we have argued above, only irrevocable stability in the human genetic material to constitute a developing individual sufficiently predisposed to receive the infusion of its human and rational soul.

Of the several considerations, then, which can be marshalled against the view that the human soul is created and infused at the time of conception, the argument from wastage does not, strictly speaking, appear to have probative force, although it is not unimpressive when added to others. The argument requiring the development of cerebral activity does not appear helped by the analogy with brain death and appears logically to be too demanding in calling for rational activity, or else unnecessary in requiring more than characteristically human cellular tissue, the genetic product resulting from the contributions of two human parents. Only the conclusions to be drawn from the facts of actual or possible twinning and combination of fertilised eggs appear to resist critical examination and to indicate that, rather than ensoulment occurring at the stage of conception, it can take place only when there is an unambiguously individual subject capable of receiving the soul by virtue of the fact that it is passing beyond the stage of simple reduplication and is beginning to ramify and diversify through the development of its bodily organs.

In the light of all these considerations it is important for the believer to be clear about what is the current official teaching of his Church on the subject, as distinct from the beliefs of individual Church members. Earlier in this chapter we observed that it is widely held that the view of ensoulment at conception is the official position of the Church today, although this has not always been the case. In point of fact, however, current Roman Catholic teaching on the time of human ensoulment is one of uncertainty. In the most recent statement on the subject, a Declaration on Abortion issued on 18th November 1974, by the Roman Congregation for the Doctrine of Faith, partly, it would appear, to counter moves in France to liberalise abortion laws, the point is made that throughout the Church's history any difference of views which may have been held on the time of ensoulment in no way weakened the unanimous agreement that abortion at any stage in pregnancy was seriously wrong. The Declaration acknowledges that in the Middle Ages 'it was commonly thought that the spiritual soul was present in the fetus only after the first two weeks', but it does not proceed to adjudicate on the matter, any more than did the Second Vatican Council, as we have seen.[9] 'This Declaration deliberately leaves aside at what moment in time the spiritual soul is infused. On this matter tradition is not unanimous and writers differ. Some assert it happens at the first instance of life, while others consider that it does not happen before the seed has taken up its position.'[10]

The Vatican Declaration does, however, point to recent work in genetics as showing 'that from the very first moment there is a fixed structure or genetic programme of this living being, namely a man, and this individual man is already equipped with all his own defined characteristics'. The statement, however, does not conclude that the human soul is also present from this 'very first moment', affirming only that 'at least it can be affirmed that modern science, even the most up-to-date, provides no support for those who advocate abortion'.[11] In drawing this rather minimal negative conclusion what the Declaration appears to be attacking is any view that the conceptus is simply a mass of fetal jelly or no more than an excrescence of the pregnant woman. It is genetically distinct and unique, a new member of the human species. When the question moves to whether this biological individual is possessed of a human soul, the Declaration, as we have seen, reserves judgement, but it does go on to state that 'it is not within the competence of biology to adjudicate on matters which are strictly philosophical and ethical, such as the question when a human person is constituted, or the legitimacy of abortion'. And it presses this point, in asserting that 'it is not for science to resolve such questions, since the existence of an immortal soul is not within its competence. The question is a philosophical one ...'.[12]

How, then, in the face of such acknowledged uncertainty, is the Vatican Declaration enabled to condemn abortion absolutely and at every stage of pregnancy? It advances two arguments, of which the first is that, in the absence of certain knowledge, abortion means taking the risk of killing an ensouled fetus or conceptus. 'It is certain that, even if one were to doubt whether the result of conception is already a human person, it is objectively a serious sin to incur the risk of committing homicide.' And 'if the infusion of the soul is judged only as probable (for the contrary will never be certain), to take its life is the same as incurring the *danger* of killing not just what it is hoped will be a man, but what is a man certainly possessed of a soul'.[13] The second line of argument is to stress the inviolability even of human life as such, irrespective of whether or not it is possessed of an immortal soul. 'Fertilisation is the beginning of the wonderful development of an individual human life whose various facilities need time for development and preparation for action.' And, 'even granted that the infusion of the soul occurs later, there is nevertheless in the fetus (as biological science establishes) incipient *human* life, which is preparing for the soul and is calling for the soul through which the nature received from the parents is perfected'.[14] In brief, it may be possible to have a human being which has not yet received a human soul infused by God, and is therefore not yet 'a human person', but which nevertheless (it is implied rather than stated) may not be destroyed on any account; and with this we may compare the teaching of Vatican II that 'life is to be protected with the utmost care from conception onwards'. On the other hand, it is at least probable that the soul is infused, and therefore a human person is present, from that moment of conception, and it is always morally wrong to act in disregard of the probability that what one is destroying in abortion at an early stage is in fact a human person.

Official Roman Catholic teaching, then, is that we cannot be absolutely certain when animation takes place, or when the conceptus or the fetus is a human person; but it may well be precisely at the moment of conception. This being so, it would be seriously wrong to destroy the fertilised ovum even then, because one might be killing a human person; and in any case, even if it were not at that stage a human person, any human being as such (even without a soul) calls for respect as being on the threshold of personhood. Faced with such official teaching, it would not be surprising if various individuals, even within the Roman Catholic Church, experienced certain dissatisfactions. Many might be perturbed that their Church's position is so nuanced in its arguments and is propounded with such niceties of distinction. It is scarcely the stuff of which robust political slogans and public campaigns are made, or which will provide a strong base for unequivocal charges of murder at early stages of pregnancy. On the other hand, it should be stressed that what doubt may be entertained about the time of infusion of the soul, and therefore the presence of human personhood, affects only the very earliest days or weeks of pregnancy. The Roman Declaration acknowledges the possibility of the alternative view of animation at the stage of nidation, which occurs within a few days of conception, and our argument based on stability and incipient diversification concentrates on the first two weeks of pregnancy, while even the view that cerebral activity is a prerequisite of personhood concentrates on the period of about eight weeks after conception, when the embryo begins to be referred to as a fetus. Not, of course, that any moral dilemmas arising from the status of the fertilised egg or embryo in those early days are negligible.

On the contrary, it is precisely there, with the development of post-coital contraceptive (or contra-nidative) procedures and with the expanding uses to which *in-vitro* fertilised ova are subjected, that advances in medical science are concentrating moral attention and often acrimonious controversy. And the dilemma for many advocates of an absolute protection of human life from the moment of conception may be between that of drawing unwarranted conclusions about the status of early life in order to present an unbreachable bulwark to be defended at all points, and that of forfeiting credibility at such an early stage to the detriment of its much more defensible position concerning later stages of pregnancy and fetal identity. In the former case, perhaps the most that could be advocated from such evidence as is available concerning the human identity of the embryo is a form of argument not unlike rule-utilitarianism, that possible exceptions, or doubtful cases, ought to be disregarded or not morally entertained in order to safeguard from inevitable erosion, or even abuse, the general principle or value which the moral rule is aiming to preserve. Such a mental device, however, depends for its success not only on general acceptance of the particular rule or value, but also on popular agreement that even legitimate exceptions will somehow endanger or erode the value in question, rather than perhaps enhancing and clarifying its significance. And in the latter case, regard for the facts of each case and evident respect for truth and differences between cases cannot legitimately be disregarded in some instances and seized upon in others without rightly incurring charges of selecting evidence in order to reaffirm preconceived ideas and moral stances.

Another source of dissatisfaction to be found in the official teaching which we are considering may arise from claims that it is outwith the competence of science, and specifically of biology, to adjudicate on matters which are strictly philosophical and which concern the existence of an immortal soul or the moment at which the human person is constituted, these being strictly philosophical questions. We may recall the recognition by Pope Pius XII of the physician's competence (alone) to determine the exact instant of death, and not just the biological death of individual organs but the cessation of 'human life'.[15] We cannot, of course, simply equate in all respects the onset of human life with its demise; but it is difficult to maintain that, if science is acknowledged to possess the ability to identify when the organism ceases to be a human person, it has nothing to contribute to identifying when it may be, or begin to be, such an entity. What is perhaps of more significance, however, is the claim that such issues are a matter for philosophy. The believer will note that no claims are made in this regard for either religion or theology, as if there were some privileged source of information accessible only to believers which might disclose the existence of an immortal soul or the precise moment at which the human person commences to exist. These questions are, apparently, for philosophical reflection and investigation. But which philosophy, or which particular tradition of human reflection? The Vatican document does not specify, nor can it appeal simply to the philosophical tradition particularly favoured for centuries in Roman Catholic doctrinal and theological teaching, that of Thomism. As we have already seen, Aquinas held firmly to a view of mediate, or delayed, infusion of the human soul; and indeed much of the philosophical reflection among Roman Catholics in recent years on the question of ensoulment may be traced to an influential article by the Fordham philosopher, Joseph F. Donceel, written in 1970 and entitled *Immediate Animation and Delayed Hominization*, in which he deploys the traditional Thomist position in contemporary terms to considerable effect.[16] Philosophical reflection, moreover, cannot take place in a factual vacuum, but must be heavily, if not exclusively, dependent on scientific observation of biological and other phenomena if any measure of truth or certainty is to be attained and communicated.

Underlying all Christian consideration of the beginning of human life, and giving rise to increasing puzzlement today, in view of the many developments in knowledge and achievement affecting that beginning, are the Christian belief in, and doctrine of, the soul. In an act of direct creation God 'infuses' the soul into each individual human being as a source of life and rational activity and as guarantor of the survival after death on the part of the human person so constituted. The origin of the individual soul has perplexed Christian thinkers from the earliest days, and some, like Origen, under Platonist influence, considered that human souls had pre-existed their bodily life and were now living out in this world the consequences of their pre-corporeal behaviour. Others, strongly influenced by Tertullian, found themselves driven to conclude that the individual soul, as well as the body, derived from the parents, in various forms of the position known as traducianism. Others, however, considered both these positions untenable and, like Augustine, found the idea of the individual's soul deriving from the parents to be totally at variance with their understanding of the immediate and individual creative activity which God performs in the origin of each human person. About Adam and Eve there was, for such thinkers, little difficulty, since God had moulded Adam from primeval 'stuff' and breathed into him the breath of life, acting in a similar manner for Eve over the material taken from Adam. In the case of their descendants, however, various Old Testament references to God's knowing and acting upon individuals in the womb before their birth clearly indicated prenatal personal existence, which could not be explained in terms of God's breathing life into them. The term which Christian theology was to favour in such cases was that God 'poured' the individual soul into the material container provided by the parents, by an individual action of 'infusion'. The term itself goes as far back as the 5th century theologian, Gennadius of Marseilles, who summed up the standard orthodox view in his *Book of Church Dogmas*, in a chapter which the mediaeval Peter Lombard was to quote in his highly influential work *The Book of the Sentences*.

As Gennadius explained:

The souls of men were not created from the beginning along with other intellectual natures, nor all at the same time, as Origen imagines. Nor were they sown along with their bodies in intercourse, as is rashly stated by the Luciferians, Cyril and some of the Latins, seeking to preserve the continuity of nature. We affirm that only the Creator of all knows the creation of the soul; that in intercourse only the body is sown, which by God's decree becomes coagulated inside the womb, and is developed and formed; and that once the body has been formed the soul is created and poured in, so that in the womb there is a living man consisting of soul and body, and what emerges alive from the womb is a man complete in human substance.[17]

The metaphor of God's thus 'infusing' the individual soul can be viewed as making two statements about human origin. The first, which was the prime aim of this theological assertion, was to explain how the individual person does not originate from its parents, but primarily from outside as a directly creative intervention on the part of God in each case. The other statement, which may be viewed more as an implication of the metaphor, envisages the physical body developing to the stage of being a suitable container into which God pours the soul as a quite distinct entity. If this distinction between body and soul is stressed, then a dualism is developed in which, following Plato and one powerful current of Christian asceticism and spirituality, the body and the physical are viewed as a constraint and a prison from which the soul must strive continuously to free itself until released in death; or, in more Cartesian terms, the body is viewed as simply a machine for the soul. If, however, the distinction between body and soul is acknowledged, but their union seen as much more than simply juxtaposition, as milk in a jug, and more in terms of bronze poured into a mould which will 'set' it in a particular shape and configuration as a statue, then a body-soul relationship is developed in Aristotelian terms of 'matter' and 'form', which yields a much more integrated view of the human individual. It was this approach, through Aquinas, which became the accepted view of man in Roman Catholic philosophical thinking. In such thinking body and soul are not two separate 'things', but more two aspects of one and the same individual human person, who is as much an ensouled body as he is an embodied soul. The soul is, as it were, the inner 'shape' of man's material composition, as a car-engine is the interrelatedness of all its components, or, perhaps, as a chord in music is something more than the simultaneous sounding of several notes.

In order to produce a chord, of course, it is necessary to be able first to produce individual notes, rather than simply undifferentiated noise or sound. And similarly, for a human person to be produced, it first appears necessary, in this way of viewing the person, for there to be a degree of development and complexity in his physical make-up which will provide not simply the necessary pre-conditions for the soul to be infused but the material constituent of the human person as such. For believers it was palaeontology rather than embryology which brought this feature of the human compositum into prominence, with increasing speculation and reflection on the process of human evolution, just as it is this explanation of the evolutionary origin of man which is viewed by some as jeopardising the direct intervention of God in the creation of the human soul. As Pope Pius XII observed in 1950, in his comments on the theory of evolution, the Church had no objection to exploring the possibility that the human body originated from pre-existing organic matter, but 'the Catholic faith bids us still to hold that souls are created immediately by God'.[18] The whole weight of this qualifying affirmation lies, of course, in the word 'immediately', as maintaining the view that the full evolutionary emergence of man as such came about by direct divine action from without, to raise man above the threshold of human consciousness, as in the traditional 'infusion' language, rather than allowing for a more thorough-going view that his human personhood 'welled up' from within as the physical organism became increasingly complex and refined. The final state in each case would be the same, but in the latter the divine activity would be more mediate, with the creation of the soul as the inner culmination of a long process initiated and sustained by God's creative action.

It is not entirely clear on what grounds Pope Pius XII declared that the immediate creation of human souls by God is a matter of Catholic faith, or belief, which must be held on to even if some moderate form of evolution is considered tenable in the case of the human body. It should be noted, of course, that 'immediate' here is not concerned with the passage of time or with the point in time at which the soul comes into existence, such as we have considered earlier in this chapter, but with the absence of intermediaries in God's creation of the soul, whether those intermediaries be considered as previous rudimentary forms of soul, or as mediating causes through which the soul comes into existence, such as Neoplatonist and Gnostic demiurges (or mediaeval angels) or even the human parents. If the human soul, being spirit, is conceived of as totally non-material, and therefore inherently simple in its constitution, then, of course, it is difficult to envisage it as appearing, as it were, by stages upon the evolutionary scene. It is this remarkable fact to which Pierre Teilhard de Chardin draws particular attention in *The Phenomenon of Man*, in the chapter entitled 'The Birth of Thought', as summed up in the new and characteristically human activity of reflection. 'The being who is the object of his own reflection, in consequence of that very doubling back upon himself, becomes in a flash able to raise himself into a new sphere. In reality, another world is born.'[19] But this threshold between animal instinct and human reflection can only have been crossed in a single critical, however apparently tiny, stride. For this Teilhard coined the word 'hominisation'.

> Man only progresses by slowly elaborating from age to age the essence and the totality of a universe deposited within him. To this grand process of sublimation it is fitting to apply with all its force the word *hominisation*. Hominisation can be accepted in the first place as the individual and instantaneous leap from instinct to thought, but it is also, in a wider sense, the progressive phyletic spiritualisation in human civilisation of all the forces contained in the animal world.[20]

In so describing and analysing what he insisted on describing as man solely as a phenomenon, de Chardin made it quite clear that he was not closing gaps or discontinuities concerning which, and to explain which, religious thought might wish to propose divine 'creative' operation or 'spiritual intervention'; and his self-denying ordinance has not been sufficiently recognised by all his critics.[21] It is to the credit, however, of another of this century's most influential Catholic thinkers, Karl Rahner, that he has directed attention to the body-soul compositum which is the human person, and to the notion of divine causal activity raised by the assertion that God 'immediately' creates human souls. In his study *Hominisation*, which considers the evolutionary origin of man as a theological problem, Rahner describes the statement of Pius XII as the official teaching of the Church, although not an actually defined doctrine.[22] (And, in any case, it cannot be considered traditional teaching, it may be added, if it is directed at a position of complete evolutionary development in man which has been current only in the past century.) Matter and spirit, he observes, cannot be totally and absolutely disparate if the God who is Spirit created matter, and did so 'essentially for the sake of spirit and as orientated towards it'. Given this kinship of some kind between matter and spirit, we are enabled to conclude that

> . . . the spiritual soul, of course, as spirit, and as form of the body, does not possess two completely different functions but in both its partial functions it has only one, namely, to fulfil its unitary nature as spirit. Consequently its corporeality is necessarily an integrating factor of its constitution as spirit, not something alien to spirit but a limited factor in the accomplishment of spirit itself.[23]

And if this is so, Rahner concludes, and

> . . . if matter and spirit are not simply disparate in nature but matter is in a certain way 'solidified' spirit, the only significance of which is to serve to make actual spirit possible, then an evolutionary development of matter towards spirit is not an inconceivable idea.[24]

What may perhaps be noted as significantly influential in this line of reflection is its positive consideration of the material as well as the spiritual in creation and in man's composition, by contrast with almost all official religious statements. In the latter, there is a frequent pre-occupation to combat an out-and-out 'materialism' which would deny any reality to other than material entities, and in the process there is, if not a depreciation of matter, at least a strong affirmation of the existence of spirit and an emphasis on the radical differences between matter and spirit. What Teilhard, to some extent, and Rahner, certainly, take placidly for granted is the existence of both matter and spirit; and in this non-polemical approach they are more at pains to explore the affinities between them than to polarise their differences. It is perhaps this welcome imperturbability in reflection which is to be seen more directly when Rahner approaches the way in which God acts as cause of human souls.

> If the operation of a creature is on principle to be regarded as a self-transcendence in such a way that the effect is not derivable from the essence of the creature acting and yet must be considered as effected by this agent, it is possible to say, without anxiety, if such a general concept of becoming and operation is presupposed,

that the parents are the cause of the one entire human being and so also of its soul, because (as we have said on the basis of the particular concept of causation which has here been worked out), that not only does not exclude, but positively includes, the fact that the parents can only be the cause of the human being in virtue of the power of God which renders possible their self-transcendence, and which is immanent in their causality without belonging to the constitutive factors of their essence.[25]

Behind such characteristically tentative, and at times tortuous, statements lies for Rahner a view that God as creator and sustainer of all created reality is at work in all causation of his creatures, working through them as his agents and instruments; and that for him to act otherwise in creation is not to be expected, as if he were envisaged as a cause simply working alongside other causes in the universe. Everything which produces an effect, he explains, brings about an increase in reality which is not reducible simply to the agent, but which must ultimately be ascribed to God as the source of all being, enabling the agent from within to 'go beyond', or transcend, itself in producing what is both its and God's effect.

As a principle method, the case seems to be that everywhere that an effect is observed in the world, a cause within the world is to be postulated and such an intra-mundane cause may and must be looked for precisely because God (rightly understood) effects everything through second causes. Consequently, to postulate or discover such a cause within the world for an effect localised in space and time within the world does not derogate in any way from the total divine causality, but is in fact necessary precisely in order to bring out sharply the absolutely unique character of God's operation as compared with any cosmic causality.[26]

For Rahner, then

... the statement that God directly creates the soul of a human being does not imply any denial of the statement that the parents procreate the human being in his unity. It makes the statement more precise by indicating that this procreation belongs to that kind of created efficient causality in which the agent by virtue of divine causality essentially exceeds the limits set by his own essence.[27]

As in the case of life itself originating from inorganic matter, so

in the case of human emergence within the evolutionary process, and in the case of each human reproduction, what is
involved may be not so much God's 'bypassing' his creatures
to intervene 'immediately' by injecting a new miracle ingre-
dient and, in the case of man, 'pouring in' a human soul, but
rather new stages and expressions of being 'welling up' from
within, through the genuine activity of created agencies
(whether inorganic or humanoid or human) which have
already reached a certain threshold of existence and are impel-
led further by the cosmic creative activity of God.

Such reflections and speculations as these are evidence of
dissatisfaction with the traditional idea of the soul as a closed,
extra-terrestrial reality which is somehow and miraculously
'added' by God to each and every human conceptus; and,
however tentative they may be, they do at least attempt to
grapple with advances in scientific knowledge and experience.
They do considerably more justice to the physical dimension
of man in such areas as heredity, sexuality and parentage. In
every case they also systematically acknowledge the significance of development and progression in human becoming, as
in many other areas of religious and theological reflection
today. And in the specific case of the status of the fertilised
ovum they converge in pointing towards a process of delayed
rather than instantaneous hominisation in the individual, no
less than, and in principle comparable with, the emergence of
man upon the evolutionary scene.

In the light of all these reflections on official Roman Catholic
teaching, as it currently stands, on the status of the fertilised
ovum and the human embryo in its early stages, we may now
consider the ethical conclusions which are drawn from that
status and form part of that teaching. The Declaration on
Abortion which we have been considering concludes, as we
have seen, that 'if the infusion of the soul [at conception] is
judged only as probable (for the contrary will never be certain),
to take its life is the same as incurring the *danger* of killing not
just what it is hoped will be a man, but what is a man certainly
possessed of a soul'. And 'it is certain that even if one were to
doubt whether the result of conception is already a human
person, it is objectively a serious sin to incur the risk of
committing homicide'.[28] It is clear that the moral force of these

statements depends heavily on the meaning to be given to such words as 'probable', 'certain', 'danger', and 'doubt' in the context being considered. It is equally clear, as a principle for elucidating these terms in a statement emanating from the conservatively-minded Roman Congregation for the Doctrine of Faith, that they are to be understood against the background of traditional Roman Catholic moral theology and the way in which that discipline handles such terms. To state, then, that we shall never attain certainty that the soul is not infused at conception, and that therefore infusion at conception will always be, at the very least, probable, is to raise questions about what sort of certainty and probability is being entertained. Absolute certainty about a state of affairs, as distinct from personal – and often fallible – conviction, is rarely achieved in human matters, and the most one can regularly hope for, as Aristotle and Aquinas realised, is certainty sufficient to justify a choice of action. It admits of degrees, as recognised in such terms as being 'practically certain', or, in a circular-sounding expression, being 'morally certain', which can be viewed as shorthand expressions for stating that there are very strong reasons indeed for holding to a particular view of affairs.

'Probability', as a technical term in moral theology, has had a long and very chequered history. In English usage, to say that something is probable is understood as expressing the view that it is more likely than not to be true, that the odds are in its favour. In the Catholic moral tradition, however, 'probable' does not entail such a comparison with the alternative, but means simply 'proveable', or indeed, 'arguable', in the sense that one or more arguments can be advanced to support it without necessarily 'proving' it in the strong sense of that term. Thus, it is perfectly possible, in this usage, to consider a particular state of affairs probable while at the same time considering the opposite equally probable, or indeed more probable. In other words, one may have one or more good reasons for thinking so, even although there may be other, and better, reasons for thinking otherwise. In the circumstances, what is one to do? How is one to resolve the 'doubt'? After decades of often acrimonious controversy (to which Pascale made his own stinging contributions), it became, and has remained, accepted in Roman Catholic moral teaching that in such dilemmas, and provided, inter alia, that no harm comes to a third party, it is morally justifiable to act upon a view of affairs which one has good reason to consider true, however strong the alternative view may be.

Of the various difficulties which such a moral doctrine raises, two may be singled out here. The first is that, historically, this school of 'probabilism' was at pains to stress that, given good reason, or a well-founded 'probability', the individual is morally permitted to choose a course of action based on that 'probability', in spite of other considerations, including legal enactments, which point in a different direction. In the Declaration on Abortion which we are considering, however, the conclusion is drawn, from a state of affairs which is grudgingly conceded as perhaps only 'probable', that there is only one moral choice available, which is to accept that probability as true and to act accordingly, however strong may be the arguments indicating otherwise. What is judged hypothetically 'only as probable' is nevertheless considered mandatory. The other weakness of probabilism in general, and its application in this context in particular, is that it makes no allowance for weighing and comparing 'probabilities', or arguments. It is not concerned with comparisons, and indeed it systematically avoids such an exercise. It may be said to be unduly individualistic, not only as concerns the responsibility of the moral agent, but even more so as concerns the identification of 'probabilities' in isolation from each other. By contrast, most moral decisions which are taken in real life essentially involve a comparing of pro's and con's, with an eye to the accumulation or convergence of arguments on both sides, and a final choice of what appears most likely, at least, to be the true state of affairs. In this view of things, what in itself may appear a 'good reason' or a probability, may come to be seen as little more than a possibility at most, with more or less likelihood of being true, particularly when compared with other considerations. In such cases, what may in the abstract be considered, in traditional moral terms, 'probable', may in actual fact be finally regarded as quite unlikely, not so much a positive consideration favouring one side as a weakness in the other side which makes it fall short of certainty.

The Declaration on Abortion considers it at least probable

that at conception the human soul is divinely infused to constitute a human person possessed of all the natural rights owing to
such a person. The force of 'probable' here is the force of the
arguments advanced in favour of such a position, which we
have already considered in their negative and positive form.
The negative line of argument, however, which argues from
the absence of any subsequent development so significant as to
indicate a qualitative change in the developing organism, to
conclude that it must have enjoyed fully personal status and a
soul from conception, turns out upon further examination to
carry little, if any, force. For, apart from considerations of
wastage, which at least may give one pause, the possibility of
twinning and recombination in every conceptus (whether it
occurs spontaneously or not) argues against a biologically
stable subject for such immediate animation. And more positively, we may now add, the paradigm of evolution of the
human species, insofar at least as it requires a process of gradual
development before hominisation, lends weight to the view
that a characteristically human soul requires characteristically
human material with which to fuse in order to constitute a fully
human person. Moreover, the human soul which constitutes
personhood is not to be envisaged as pure spirit poured into a
biological receptacle at conception, but more properly is seen
as welling up from within the joint material provided by the
parents in a genuine exercise of causation of the total human
composite on their part, without invoking additional and
almost miraculous intervention on the part of God other than
his creative action in the production of all fresh reality. Thus,
the affinity which exists between matter and spirit permits, and
almost appears to require, one to view the emergence of a new
human person as a process which requires time and some
measure of pre-personal existence (in the strict sense) as a
threshold from which the leap to fully animated existence may
be launched.

The conclusion to this would be that the negative argument
urged in favour of immediate animation carries no force, and
that all the weight of this position must then fall on the single
positive argument from increased knowledge of human
genetics. As the Vatican Declaration expresses it, the science of
genetics 'has shown that from the very first moment there is a

fixed structure or genetic programme of this living being, namely, a man, and this individual is already equipped with all his own defined characteristics'.[29] What the Declaration does not assert is that this living being is a human person (it deliberately, as we have seen, leaves this question open). The most it appears to claim is that it 'probably' is, since the contrary can never be proved. To entertain, however, even the possibility that there can be for a period of time a living human being, or a living human entity, which does not possess a human soul and is not therefore a human person, is a major concession, which, however, raises many questions concerning the status of this non-ensouled, non-personal, human entity. It cannot, for one thing, have any rights, since traditional Catholic doctrine holds that rights flow from the status of being a person. It appears, in fact, to be none other than human tissue. It is undoubtedly alive; it is clearly of human origin; and it is genetically unique, both as human and as individually human, in the sense that there is none other like it. Given appropriate favourable circumstances for development, of course, it will, in due time, develop into an 'ensouled' being and therefore a human person. And that inherent potential would appear to distinguish it from any other piece of human tissue, were it not for the fact that the possibility of cloning, or inserting the nucleus of any human cell into an enucleated ovum, uncovers this potential in all human tissue. It may well be that the status of this living being on the way to hominisation is comparable in significant ways to the status of primates (to go back no further) at a pre-human stage in the evolution of *homo sapiens*, as we now identify that evolutionary process.

It appears, then, that neither the negative nor the positive arguments for immediate ensoulment at conception have probative value, and that the case for a process of organic development leading to that flowering of personhood is a quite impressively strong one. In the circumstances, it appears that the most one can conclude of the 'probability' that ensoulment occurs at conception is that it is possible but, when all is taken into account, rather unlikely. What then becomes of the ethical consequences deriving from the status of the fertilised ovum and the embryo in its early stages of development? And to what degree would one who destroyed such a being be incurring the risk of committing homicide, as the Vatican Declaration asserts? There is no doubt, of course, that one would be destroying something which is alive, but the question is, is it more than live human tissue? The degree of moral risk corresponds to the degree of likelihood that what one is dealing with is an ensouled human person. Accordingly, if one considers it just possible, but quite unlikely, that one is faced with a human person, the risk that in destroying it one is deliberately killing or destroying such a person must be considered correspondingly slight.

The Vatican Declaration does not consider the question of degrees of likelihood and therefore of risk, stating simply that 'it is objectively a serious sin to incur the risk of committing homicide'. And yet the question is surely pertinent, how realistic is the risk in question? No less pertinent must be consideration of what other factors might justify one in incurring such a risk. The closest to which traditional moral theology came to discussing this type of situation was in exemplifying theories of action in doubtful cases by considering that of the huntsman in a forest shooting at a moving object as it emerged from a thicket, regardless of whether it was a deer or a man. The parallel with the situation we are here considering is quite illuminating, not only in pinpointing attention on a deliberately life-destroying action directed at a living object whose identity is in doubt, but also in helping to clarify under what circumstances such behaviour would be morally justifiable. Three such circumstances appear particularly relevant in each case: the degree of care taken to eliminate the likelihood or the possibility that the object in the thicket is in fact not a man; the motive of the hunter, whether he is simply out shooting for 'pleasure' or whether, for example, at the other end of the scale, his own survival or that of others depends on his securing a supply of food; and the correlation between the degree of likelihood and the degree of necessity. From such considerations it is not unreasonable to conclude that, if one is satisfied beyond reasonable doubt that the human conceptus is not yet so developed as to be an ensouled human person, and if one's purpose in bringing about its destruction is sufficiently capable of moral scrutiny, then to do so is not, even objectively, morally blameworthy.

Might it not be argued, however, that if one is satisfied beyond reasonable doubt that the conceptus does not yet possess a human soul and is not yet therefore a human person, then what one does with it, and for whatever motive, has no more moral significance than what one does with any fragment of human tissue or of the human organism, such as skin or blood or, for that matter, kidney? The Vatican Declaration on Abortion observes that 'even granted that the infusion of the soul occurs later, there is nevertheless in the fetus (as biological science establishes) incipient *human* life, which is preparing for the soul and calling for the soul through which the nature received from the parents is perfected'.[30] That such life is human, as the Declaration stresses, is not in itself any more morally significant than that all human tissue is genetically human. What adds particular moral significance, however, is that it is not only human but also 'incipient' human life. It is not a person, in this hypothesis, and cannot therefore possess any of the human rights, including the basic right to life, which derive from human personhood. Some might wish to suggest a parallel with the case of animals, which, if they cannot be said to possess rights, may nevertheless be considered as having 'interests', as we shall discuss in the next chapter. Much more significant, however, appears to be the fact that, unlike animals, the unensouled fetus has promise, which may be considered a much more expressive term than 'potential', at least in English. Earlier we drew a comparison of sorts between the unensouled fetus and the race of primates before the critical emergence of fully human status in the evolutionary process. If by some biological or environmental mishap that race of primates had been wiped out, and the threshold to reflection had not therefore been crossed, what Teilhard identified as the noösphere would not have come into existence, and the evolutionary promise which we now see was present in the pre-human stage would have been tragically unfulfilled.

From our experimental point of view, reflection is, as the word indicates, the power acquired by a consciousness to turn in upon itself, to take possession of itself *as of an object* endowed with its own particular consistence and value: no longer merely to know, but to know oneself; no longer merely to know, but to know that one knows ... Now the consequences of such a transformation are immense, visible as clearly in nature as any of the facts recorded by physics or astronomy. The being who is the object of his own reflection, in consequence of that very doubling back upon himself, becomes in a flash able to raise himself into a new sphere. In reality, another world is born. Abstraction, logic, reasoned choice and inventions, mathematics, art, calculation of space and time, anxieties and dreams of love – all these activities of *inner life* are nothing else than the effervescence of the newly-formed centre as it explodes onto itself.[31]

Something comparable on an individual scale may be said to be the promise and the loss involved in the disintegration and death of the human fetus in its earliest stages. And to this the believer would wish to add, with St Paul, that what is in preparation is the body as temple of the Holy Spirit and the human person imaged after God and befriended by his all-encompassing love. To deprive a being of such a future, and to interrupt the passage to personhood upon which it is embarked, cannot be homicide. We have argued that it is, in fact, unlikely to be possessed of a soul and personhood in its existence at the simple cell-multiplication stage prior to diversification. The obverse, however, of this argument is that, once that stage has been passed and diversification towards human organs has begun to occur, then we probably are in the presence of a human person in its embryonic state of development; and that, as development increases rapidly, so also does the likelihood of homicide as an accurate description of any action which terminates its existence. Even in the very earliest days, moreover, such an action could not responsibly be undertaken for any but most serious reasons, going far beyond considerations of convenience or scientific curiosity, and affecting either that being's own prospects for the future, as in cases of genetic abnormality, or the life and welfare of others, as in cases of rape and incapacity in a woman to carry a child to term without risk to herself.

In the previous chapter we have drawn attention to the sheer mystery of human existence, and in this we have explored something of its mysterious origins. Sheer respect for being in all its manifestations, and particularly for the wonder of our being in its physical as well as its spiritual manifestations, should be one of the hallmarks of that world of human reflection which de Chardin so eloquently described as the characteristic of man, and well justifies the exhortation of the Second Vatican Council that 'life is to be protected with the utmost care from conception onwards'.[32] Reflection on the status of such life in its several stages of development, which the Council of set purpose did not consider, leads us to conclude that it is possible with a fair measure of moral certainty to maintain that human personhood cannot be ascribed to it in its earliest stages of development, but that the intrinsic promise which it does contain even then cannot be thereby discounted or simply disregarded. If it cannot in strict accuracy be said with reference to the early embryo, 'this is when *I* began' as an individual personal subject, it can nevertheless be claimed that 'from this biological matrix, I as a person, took my origin'.

4

Medical Research and Experimentation

The various issues in medicine whose moral implications we have been considering in this study are issues which arise largely from the remarkable progress in medical science which we have all witnessed in recent decades. Questions which are raised for moral and religious consideration in the field of human fertility control, both positive and negative, in the final span of our earthly existence which we call dying and death, and in the remarkable expansion of possibilities connected with the very beginning of life, are all questions which in the short term refer to the ethical application of new discoveries and techniques, and in the long term stir up more profound and fundamental questions about individual human life in the society of other such individuals within a material environment, about its purpose and about its final individual and collective destiny. These questions would not have arisen, at least in the increasingly urgent form which they assume today, without significant advances in medical science; and these advances would not have been achieved in medical, as in any science, without research and experimentation. It is appropriate, then, by way of rounding off the major topics which we have been considering, to direct attention to the conditions which have so often raised them in acute form, and which also in their own right raise issues to which morality and belief must address themselves.

In the circumstances, this also is a useful context in which to consider what is to be understood by the term morality, this also being a discipline of thought and life which contains within itself considerable scope for research and experimentation. Ethics, or Christian or theological ethics, or (in more

Catholic terminology) moral theology, may be briefly described as a discipline which attempts to provide a coherent and consistent system of thought within which to identify and direct various human aspirations, options and choices. It does not create moral experience, the human experience of obligation, the interior feeling of being under obligation or under claim to perform certain actions or abstain from certain other actions. It seeks to examine this unique and irreducible moral experience and to assess it, identifying and perhaps filtering out elements explainable in other terms, such as inherited and environmental influences, purely social conventions or pressures, and emotional considerations. The raw material with which the discipline works appears to be human attitudes and actions and their relationship towards certain values, such as human flourishing, freedom, truth, beauty, integrity, love and, for the believer, the being of God. The precise meaning and import of each of these values, and others, is, of course, warmly contested within the discipline, as also is any hierarchy or priority to be established among them when they are, or appear to be, in conflict. A major debate about them is whether they are simply human inventions, mental constructs of purely factual experience; that is, whether we invent our values and impose them upon reality; or whether, by contrast, we discover and identify them already in reality and in our experience of reality, responding to them as precious elements or veins to be mined and so brought to light.

On the whole, the believer who accepts God as creator and craftsman, and who accepts the fundamental truth of the Book of Genesis that when God looked upon his completed handiwork, 'behold, it was good, it was very good', will approach all reality with respect and reverence, in the conviction that such reality is instinct, or permeated, with values. He will view his vocation, or commission, as one of continuing the 'good' work of creativity, as God's invitation to him, which is the moral experience, to cooperate and collaborate in discovering and expressing moral values wherever they are to be found. Man, in brief, is a moral prospector. As Jesus said, 'The kingdom of heaven is like a merchant looking for fine pearls. When he finds one of great value he goes and sells everything he owns and buys it' (Mt 13:45–46).

It may be taken as axiomatic that man is, at heart, a searcher. That brilliant thinker, the North African bishop of Hippo, St Augustine, who was possessed of an incredibly enquiring mind (as well as of an incredibly depressing view of human sexuality) wrote of the restlessness of the human heart, and he could have added, of the human mind. As a theologian, he saw this as ultimately man's innate thirst for God, the water of life, but also as a continuing quest for values and as a profoundly human characteristic. That quest and pursuit is man's birthright, and as our awareness of the reality about us, and within us, increases, it inevitably leads to diversification and increasing specialisation, as every scientist knows. Such a development of more and more refined concentration of resources and energies upon one aspect of reality, or one branch of science, is an absolute condition of success and of ever fresh discoveries and developments. But by the same token it incurs corresponding dangers, if that is not too strong a term. First, we may suggest, it raises for the individual engaged in such activity, and for his or her personal life, questions about the scale of values, or the priorities operative in his life and work, and the personal balance to be struck in that scale between, for example, work, health, companionship, dependents, general culture and, the believer would add, adherence to religious values. It is clear that no blue-print can be applied to everyone, and what is already at issue here is the series of personal moral choices which ultimately only each individual can make for himself or herself. Moreover, it appears to be a characteristic of any specialist in his field that he is willing and prepared to sacrifice certain aspects and dimensions of his life in favour of others. That being so, the question must arise of his motives in making such sacrifices, which, even if they are not experienced as sacrifices by him, may well be sacrifices which he is asking of others, and particularly his dependents.

In thus raising the question of motives which lead to engaging in research and experimentation, we may acknowledge the ordinary legitimate ones of earning a living, of job-satisfaction commensurate with one's talents, and of personal ambition, just as we may take for granted attitudes of honesty, loyalty and integrity, in a word, the normal professional canons and standards. What may here be singled out are the reasons why a particular line of research and experimentation is engaged upon, and these may be taken to be either the disinterested quest for knowledge or the desire to see it applied in beneficent ways in society, or a mixture of both.

If we consider first the search for fresh knowledge and information it is possible to distinguish between these two terms by stating that 'information' can be defined as relevant knowledge. What may be jokingly referred to as 'today's piece of useless information' is really a free-floating item of knowledge which appears to contribute nothing to the matter in question or the business in hand. It is not relevant; or, in more ominous terms, it does not contribute to the expansion of industry or the increase in the gross national product or even to human wellbeing and flourishing. Such demand for relevance is, of course, the bane of the pure researcher; and he is right to resist it and be suspicious of it. Not just, however, because it is a restraint on his freedom of free and disinterested enquiry, but because his scientific activity, simply as human activity, puts critical questions to the very meaning and implied restraints of 'relevance', lifting it out of foreshortened perspectives of immediate or short-term advantages of a material or economic character to locate it within the broader and richer context of the human spirit's appropriation of knowledge and truth which we broadly call culture. To quote Augustine again, he envisaged heaven as the fulfilment and satisfaction of all human searching and as including the facility of being able just to relax and look, to contemplate the sheer beauty of truth, which he found personified in the Christian God. In more mundane terms, but in the same current of respect for enquiry as a human birthright, Aristotle was of the view that the unexamined life is unworthy of a human being. And with all our contemporary problems of world recession, of political tension between east and west, and of gross imbalance of wealth between north and south, the quality of really human living simply demands that some place must always be found for individuals and activities which an economist such as Adam Smith might term 'unproductive', but whose absence from any society constitutes either a fundamental human impoverishment or a stultification of the human spirit.

This is not to deny, of course, that in any society at a given time certain restraints or limitations are inevitable, whether of financial resources or of competing claims or priorities; and the problems of striking balances constitute a continuing challenge to any human community in its day-to-day decisions as, at a deeper level, in its understanding of the function of any society. Nor is it to deny that there are restraints of a deeper and equally human nature to be considered and recognised as affecting the pursuit of knowledge and scientific truth. For the pursuit of truth and knowledge cannot be an absolute value, but is hedged about by other values, and notably by that of respect for persons, which the believer would also wish to identify as love. Not only 'speaking the truth in love', as the letter to the Ephesians exhorts (4:15), but also seeking it and applying it, is the fundamental moral restraint and qualification which, the believer especially would claim, should characterise all scientific research and experimentation. Enquiry into pain and its effects, for instance, and establishing the tolerance degree of animals or human beings, does not ipso facto justify all infliction of pain. Certainly no Jew would ever subscribe to that proposition. And some knowledge or information can be 'tainted', like dirty money, by the methods employed to acquire it, as may be the case, for instance, in some areas of sexual behaviour and sex-therapy. Not that the knowledge acquired is itself in some sense morally wrong, and once acquired it has become part of the human treasury; but that it carries with it an element of moral distastefulness from the manner in which it was achieved, such that one would be morally entitled to say that, if it could be acquired in no other way, then it would be humanly and morally preferable not to have achieved it. The infliction of torture in order to secure important information may be considered a typical example.

Another example, of more medical pertinence, which aroused considerable public disquiet some years ago, and resulted in governmental enquiry in Britain, was disclosure of the fact that dead human fetuses resulting from induced abortions were being sold and used for research purposes. Laying aside the distaste for the mercenary aspects of the practice, the conclusion to which an opponent of abortion would come is of deploring that research material should have come to hand in such a manner. It would, nevertheless, be both impracticable and unreasonable for such a person to decline to profit, or have others profit, from the knowledge thus acquired; and indeed he might view such knowledge as at least some positive good resulting for others from what otherwise could be nothing more than a tragic waste of human life.

One moral restraint, then, upon research and experimentation must be what is basically a human and scientific respect for the raw material of such enterprises, comparable to the respect (and, the believer would add, reverence) of any artist for the medium in which he works. In the case of humans, such respect must take the form of specific recognition of their rights and liberties, their physical, emotional and spiritual integrity, and especially their capacity for the rational exercise of freedom, in which many believers would see that aspect of man which constitutes in him the image of the God who created him.

Another moral consideration which must enter in at some stage is the use to which results will be put, or are intended to be put, which is not always necessarily the same thing. Some scientific information is acquired almost by accident, of course, rather than by design, as was outstandingly exemplified in Fleming's discovery of penicillin. Other information is more the result of a project pursued with single-minded persistence in terms of specific information sought rather than knowledge as such. And perhaps here the outstanding instance is the work of Rutherford and others on atomic structure. Success in achieving the release of atomic energy latent in matter may be seen today as one of the most humanly ambiguous achievements of scientific research and experimentation. Few would deny the potentially cataclysmic effects of a nuclear explosion, while some would also consider the simple capacity to achieve it, in terms of deterrence, as affording man a positive, if precarious, instrument for maintaining international peace and order. At a lesser point of urgency, some would see in the peaceful harnessing of nuclear power a heaven-sent resource to replace dwindling and inefficient forms of fossil-fuel, while others are more impressed by the dangers concomitant with such development.

This type of consideration raises moral questions which do not vainly attempt to brand new discoveries or procedures in science as morally bad, but which are rather directed at the human capacity to absorb new developments and at society's need to be able to control their timing, whether in allocating resources, or in imposing moratoria (as in the case of genetic engineering), or even in closing particular avenues of research as either unwanted or premature. What this argues for is considerable more thought on the part of society, including scientists, about the positive directions and negative controls, undertaken in good time, which may be required as a social and human environment within which to locate research and experimentation projects which are severally directed at human betterment and which therefore may require to be evaluated within a more comprehensive view of such individual and collective betterment. And it is here, of course, that legislation and international conventions and agreements call for further development. At the same time, it is realistic to acknowledge that to speak of 'society' is to ignore the deep political and ideological rifts which exist within humankind and which result in antagonisms and rivalries between nations. It is equally realistic to recognise in such fields as medicine and drug development the existence of vast private as well as public resources and the degree to which commercial and profit considerations are operative in all research and experimentation. And it is no less realistic to concede that science is in principle irrepressible, and at times quite unpredictable. Perhaps, then, the most that one can hope for, as well as the least that one can do, is to encourage and stimulate and engage in widespread discussion to influence and inform public opinion on at least the major issues and implications arising from research and experimentation in various fields of medicine, as well as those occasioned by these activities themselves and their pursuit, and in the process to identify considerations and values which might form a basis, if agreed upon, for either voluntary or imposed restraint in such areas as research and experimentation. In exploring such a possibility it may be useful to consider the various types of subjects of such activities, and to examine such considerations as may be relevant, commencing with animals and proceeding to unreflective humans, to conclude with adult free individuals.

There is much disquiet today about various forms of animal

husbandry, and also considerable revulsion experienced over the hounding of animals to death for human enjoyment. There is also much opposition, of a more or less active nature, to the whole concept of animal experimentation and to the pain and suffering inflicted upon animals in the name of human betterment. The difficult questions to be faced here are to what degree, if any, we are justified in exploiting animals in the cause of human betterment, and whether various attempts at justification do not, rather, throw in doubt whether or not the ultimate aims really do achieve a human betterment of man's situation. Some people would see in animals fellow living creatures of God to be respected, and would reject any justification in human terms of pain inflicted on animals as simply an assertion of supremacy on the part of the stronger human species. Others would regard animals rather as the byways and cul de sacs of biological evolution on its onward march to the emergence of man. Others again wonder in exasperation what all the bother is about, and might point to the enormous amount of human suffering which is crying out for alleviation, and indeed some of which can be alleviated as a result of animal experimentation. More recently, some people would wish to maintain that animals too, and not just humans, possess rights not to be destroyed or assaulted and not to be subjected to intolerable conditions, but to have their integrity and freedom respected and fostered. To others, however, this ascribing of rights to animals on the grounds of sentience appears a novel and unjustified departure from the more traditional approach which sees natural rights as applicable only to human beings, not only on account of what specifically differentiates man from even the higher animals, his power of reflective choice, but also on account of the traditional connection between rights and duties in one and the same individual. Many believers in particular would wish to maintain that rights and duties are two sides of a coin, such that the human person's rights to life, liberty and the pursuit of happiness, for instance, and the claims which they may enable him to make upon others, are not simply ends in themselves but enable him, or will in time enable him, to live and act as a responsible agent, towards God primarily, but also towards his neighbour and himself. And if animals cannot exercise moral responsibility in free and

94

rational choice, as they manifestly cannot, this argument would run, then they cannot be said, in any moral sense of the word, to possess rights.

Perhaps a less contentious and startling approach is to be found in recognising that at least animals have interests, granted that one is disposed to distinguish between rights and interests in any subject, and that the question of animal experimentation is one of balancing the interests of animals against the interests of mankind. That some such balancing as a means of justifying pain inflicted on animals appears to be involved may be concluded from the fact that very many people do, in fact, feel that the infliction of pain on animals calls for some moral justification. And at the very least such an attempt at balancing does concentrate attention on the distress which is being caused and at the same time prompts scrutiny of the human interests adduced to justify the inflicting of such distress. Thus, to come to cases, to submit animals to living in circumstances which cause considerable suffering to them in the interest of the fashion industry, or to inflict notable pain on them in the interest of male or female cosmetics, cannot be morally justifiable. Evaluation becomes more complex when such experimentation is conducted for the purpose of genuine human betterment, in testing drugs or new medical or surgical techniques. But it appears that over-experimentation is a regular feature in many such tests, whether it be undertaken to confirm the obvious, or the by now obvious, as in the hazards of tobacco smoking, or as an ultra safety measure to meet standards which may be set too high, or to insure against possible litigation in the event of harmful effects on humans. Alternatives to such experimentation, even if more expensive in financial terms to the consumer, also need to be regularly and thoroughly canvassed; and the genuine contribution of experiment on animals to curing various ailments of humans, including cancer, needs to be constantly assessed. When, however, such experimentation is judged to be of positive and indispensable value to human betterment, then the least one may morally expect is that it be kept to the lowest possible, that the degree and duration of suffering be scrupulously justified, and that Home Office requirements be continually monitored. In this field also, it is possible for information to be tainted, and for society to prefer that it not be acquired or sought if there is no alternative and more morally acceptable way.

Experimentation on humans carries with it the same moral requirements as we have seen in the case of animals, with significant additions. We have already to some extent covered the case of tissue obtained from dead fetuses, which appears to raise no moral difficulties but may occasion profound regret at some of the human actions which have resulted in the availability of such material. The question of live humans in the early stages of their existence, and experimentation on fertilised ova or early embryos, raises once again the important issue of their moral status, which we have already considered at some length. In a context of considerable public disquiet at the news of experimentation being conducted and contemplated on live human embryos the British Medical Research Council issued guidelines for research related to human fertilisation and embryology, which it considered to be generally valid for all such research, and which are interesting for a variety of reasons.[1] The statement recalled previous approval, in the pursuit of 'scientifically sound research', of work on *in-vitro* fertilisation 'where there was no intent to transfer the embryo to the uterus', and now made explicit reference to experimentation in its judgement that

> ... scientifically sound research involving experiments on the processes and products of *in-vitro* fertilisation between human gametes is ethically acceptable and should be allowed to proceed on condition both that there is no intent to transfer to the uterus any embryo resulting from or used in such experiments and also that the aim of the research is clearly defined and directly relevant to clinical problems ...

If the position may be sustained with which we concluded the previous chapter, that the early human embryo can with reasonable certainty be described as a human organism not yet sufficiently stable to possess the human soul and be identified as a person, but nonetheless charged with remarkable promise for the future, then it might be possible to conclude that the sacrifice of such promise could be justified in the interests, not just of 'pure' research (if such there be), but of other human beings, whether now fully alive or as yet non-existent. From a

species or an evolutionary standpoint, the production of fertilised ova or of embryos still at the cell-duplication stage may be
viewed as the biological continuum of human life expressing
itself in certain nodal or focal points, similar to buds on a tree.
If allowed to develop uninterruptedly, they will become
increasingly individualised and eventually hominised in the full
sense. But while still at this incipient stage prior to individuation, and a fortiori to hominisation, they may be considered as
at the service of human life itself and of its biological ameliora-
tion in fully formed individuals of the species. From the standpoint of belief, and the traditional doctrine of the creation and
infusion of the human soul, the destruction of such biologically human 'nodes' does not entail the destruction of a human
person. Nor does it entail the 'frustration' of divine creative
activity or of a human soul, for the latter simply does not yet
exist and is not, so to speak, waiting in the wings to be
embodied, as Origen speculated. Its creation and 'infusion' are
simultaneous, according to more orthodox traditional belief.

While such considerations may be granted, so far as concerns the present status of the embryo, a morally significant
factor in its present fate, we have also argued, is its inherent
promise for the future giving rise to future rights and present
interests. If even animal experimentation should be qualified
by respect for the interests of such animals, should it not
follow, at least equally, for incipient humans? It may be
argued, however, that respect for the interests of animals
appears to be directed exclusively at not inflicting pain or
suffering on them, and that such considerations cannot apply
to the human before the capacity to experience pain exists
through the development of a nervous system. What respect
appears called for in regard to the human embryo is a respect
permitting or enabling it to continue in uninterrupted existence
in its inherent progress towards personhood. Nonetheless,
what appears very elusive to grasp is the moral purchasing
power simply of promise as such. Regret at what might have
been is a common human experience, and sorrow at the death
of a young person is frequently compounded by a sense of lost
fulfilment or of disappointment at the quenching of promise
for the future. To prevent a person from coming into being is
too 'real' a description of not allowing an embryo to develop,

97

for the 'person' is purely imaginary.

In this respect it may be legitimate to draw a parallel with a married couple who decide, for whatever reasons, not to conceive and produce a child and who may, in later life, regret that decision, and speculate on how such a child would have developed and grown. From such a later viewpoint it might be legitimate to conclude with regret that the couple 'should' have had a child, but it appears very difficult to maintain that 'should' here has a strong moral sense and that they were at the time morally obliged to have a child, particularly if they then had good reasons for deciding otherwise. In such a case, 'should' appears really equivalent to 'it would have been nice', and expresses only disappointment and regret that circumstances did not permit it. Perhaps, then, one may conclude that, given sufficient reason, it is morally justifiable to decide not to bring a child into existence even from a fertilised egg or what we have termed a human biological node, however regrettable one may consider this in view of 'what might have been'. In this line of argument, experimentation on embryos which is 'directly relevant to clinical problems', as the Medical Research Council stipulates, may be seen as contributory to human biological life and to the wellbeing of such individuals as do develop. And in its own way, although it is certainly not claimed that such was in the mind of the Second Vatican Council, such activity in the interests of human life as such and of the persons who will thereby benefit may fairly be considered, it may be suggested, to be in accord with, or to be an extended interpretation of, the Council's urging that from conception onwards life should be treated with the utmost respect.[2]

It scarcely needs pointing out that the argumentation of the previous paragraph is of a markedly tentative nature, and it will be not in the least surprising if many find it inconclusive or implausible, preferring to take a stronger stand on the inviolability of the fertilised egg or human embryo, even should it not be a fully fledged person. And it is interesting to contrast the MRC guidelines on research and experimentation on human embryos with the forthright condemnation of such work made by Pope John Paul II in October 1982 in an address which he delivered in English to a gathering of biologists in Rome to discuss biological experimentation. The Pope had repeated his belief 'that science should always be accompanied and guided by the wisdom that belongs to the permanent spiritual heritage of humanity, and which is inspired by the design of God inscribed in creation, before being subsequently proclaimed by his Word'. As the Church is called to 'foster the progress of man', so also for science man is 'the ultimate term of scientific research, the whole man, spirit and body, even if the immediate object of the sciences that you profess is the body with all its organs and tissues'. He saw much to be welcomed which furthered 'the integral well-being of man', ranging from the production of new food supplies to feed the world's hungry to the work of *in-vitro* fertilisation of animals and the cultivation of animal cells and tissues aimed at treating and eradicating genetic or chromosomic diseases in children and modifying the genetic code as a praiseworthy treatment of inherited abnormalities. His strongest words, however, were reserved for experimentation on human embryos, a topic which had recently occupied the world's press. 'I condemn, in the most explicit and formal way, experimental manipulations of the human embryo, since the human being, from conception to death, cannot be exploited for any purpose whatsoever.'[3]

It may appear that, in taking so absolute a stand against experiment on the human embryo in its earliest stage, Pope John Paul was, in effect, repeating and confirming the view of immediate animation which we have considered in the previous chapter. There may also be other considerations at work, such as a strong view of human solidarity opposed to all forms of human exploitation of fellow human beings, whatever their stage of development or dissolution. It was noticeable, and perhaps morally significant, that much media and public reaction in general to announcements that experiments were being conducted on human embryos, regardless of how accurate such reports may have been in individual cases, was one of serious disquiet, which could perhaps be interpreted as a shrinking from any move towards transgressing a frontier of respect for the human species as such and towards considering some specimens as expendable in the interests of others. To argue that such embryos could be construed as having an interpretative willingness to be of service through experimentation to the wellbeing of other human individuals, on a parallel with attempts to justify non-therapeutic experimentation on children, as we shall consider next, appears altogether too fanciful a collection of hypotheses. And in any case, some embryos have no choice, even hypothetical, in the matter: they are created to be eventually destroyed, and for no other purpose.

The question returns, however, of the status of the early embryo, and what at least may be apparent is that the traditionally Christian philosophical and theological doctrine of the human soul is in a thoroughly unsatisfactory state, particularly in the light of advances in embryological studies. Postulated by Greek philosophers to account for personal unity and continuity, it was appropriated, sometimes in its Platonic and at other times in its Aristotelian form, by Christian thinkers as the spiritual principle in each individual man (and woman) which is directly infused into material 'stuff' as the unifying, organising principle of action and identity in this earthly life, but which survives bodily death to continue in existence, first for a 'time' in an unembodied state, and after 'the resurrection of the dead' in a re-embodied state for all eternity. What may be inferred is that, while such a doctrine of the soul may give a comparatively satisfying explanation of human identity and continuity in the course of our earthly life span, it encounters severe difficulties in trying to account for the commencement and the termination of that life span. And unfortunately it is at precisely those points that it, and religious belief, are being increasingly confronted by developments in medical science.

Those, however, who are prepared to accept the traditional doctrine, for all its difficulties, as better than any alternative for offering some explanation of the religious beliefs of personal creation and personal immortality, and particularly those who adopt the strong view of embryonic status, will take similar objection to the practice of creating surplus embryos, if those which are not, in the event, required for reimplantation or which are considered unsuited to transfer, are judged fit material for experimentation. It might be possible, by moral analysis as delicate as any surgical procedure, to apply even at this embryonic stage the traditional distinction between killing and letting die in the case of defective or other embryos where a major problem is that of securing their survival, and to distinguish also, so far as this may be possible, between observation of such embryos and direct experimental intervention which is of its nature destructive of their life. In the case of other, healthier embryos, rather than see them destroyed, for however laudable motives, such an approach of wellnigh absolute respect for the embryonic life would presumably prefer that they be offered for implantation and survival to another infertile woman of a childless marriage. And finally, even if those who maintain a strong view on the status of the early embryo will derive little comfort from the Medical Research Council directive that 'human ova fertilised with human sperm should not be cultured *in-vitro* beyond the implantation stage', those, on the other hand, who would regard the implantation stage as one at which the embryo is not yet sufficiently diversified to be a personal being may have less moral difficulty over such a guideline, and indeed will welcome the limitation which it places upon embryonic experimentation, even for scientifically sound and beneficent research purposes.

In the Medical Research Council statement it is interesting to note the sensitivity evidenced about the need for consent in all experimental projects upon the fertilised ovum. In no case may research be conducted on ova or sperm, or on fertilised ova which turn out to be surplus to implantation requirements, without the informed consent of the donor or donors. And it is here, perhaps, in the area of informed and explicit consent, and in the matter of ownership of human gametes and the transfer of such ownership, that society may most effectively control by legislation not only the uses to which such material may be directed in research and the availability of such material, but also the sources from which the gametes are obtained and the legitimacy of donor provision of semen or ova for extra-marital fertilisation procedures, as we have earlier suggested.[4]

The subject of consent, however, directs consideration to a further field of research and experimentation, and introduces new considerations when such experimentation is conducted upon children and other human individuals who may be incapable of giving their consent to it. It is in such cases that particular importance needs to be accorded to the standard distinction made between experimentation which is therapeutic, or undertaken in the immediate interests of the subject, and experimentation which is non-therapeutic, or directed at more long-term and far-reaching findings. The distinction is not clear-cut, of course, since non-therapeutic experiments on a particular person may eventually prove of benefit to him also, but the main point of the distinction is to identify whether a projected treatment will deliver short-term alleviation of the subject's present condition and the immediacy of such an effect. Given such a distinction, it is clear that therapeutic experimentation carries with it fewer ethical difficulties than does non-therapeutic in cases where the subject is unable to express a personal opinion or to give informed consent to the treatment envisaged. At the same time, there are obvious moral considerations involved in the choosing of a particular procedure on behalf of such a patient, who may be too young to appreciate all that is involved, or senile or otherwise mentally incapable, or simply unconscious as a result of a road accident. It is obvious, for instance, from the very meaning of the distinction that therapeutic experimentation is undertaken not simply in the interests of the patient, but in his best interests; for otherwise the choice of such treatment would include an element of non-therapeutic experimentation, and thus require a different type of decision on his part. By the same token, the experimental treatment contemplated, by virtue of being an experiment, carries with it an element of ignorance as to the outcome of such treatment, and may therefore be undertaken in the best interests of the patient only when it is clear that more established, tried and tested, forms of treatment are, for some reason, unsuitable in this case. A third consideration, which such experimental treatment shares with any other form of treatment, is the need at least to attempt to estimate the benefits hoped for from such a procedure, and to offset them against risks involved, undesirable side-effects, or the over-all final state of the patient which will result, and which may not be so significantly improved as to warrant either the side-effects or any distress or discomfort involved in the treatment itself.

It is clear that all such considerations are a matter of often the most delicate clinical judgement and experience, and that therefore the final decision to proceed or not is one which carries serious responsibilities concerning the patient, and which at best only the patient, as the person most intimately affected and concerned, can take, as has been earlier considered in our discussion of the process of dying. Failing ability to give or withhold such consent, however, it may be useful to distinguish between the alternatives of 'interpretative consent' and 'constructive consent' as justifications for another to take the decision on his behalf, while bearing in mind that at this stage we are concerned only with projected therapeutic experimentation. Both constructive consent and interpretative consent may be seen as forms of presumed consent which is resorted to in the absence of actual consent on the part of the patient, but they differ in respect of how they are reached. Constructive consent may be considered as the decision which any reasonable person would make in the given circumstances and in his own best interests, and is most obviously apparent in the case of young children who have never given thought to such situations. By contrast, interpretative consent is based on acquaintance with a specific individual and his previous history, and is an attempt to interpret what his mind and decision would be in the circumstances to hand in the light of that acquaintance. Both forms of consent are conjectural, of course, but in the absence of interpretative consent, or grounds for such more personal consent, it appears reasonable, and indeed morally mandatory, to proceed by way of constructive consent. It also appears morally required, however, out of respect for the patient, that such consent, constructed on the basis of how reasonable persons may be expected to behave, should yield to what specific knowledge is available about this particular individual and therefore to what may be reasonably conjectured would be his personal decision, subject only to the requirements of the law.

Respect for the inherent dignity of the individual human person, even when or if he is mistaken, or even perhaps especially when or if he is mistaken, appears to be of paramount consideration even in the matter of therapeutic experimentation, but it becomes of even more importance when attention is directed to the whole field of non-therapeutic experimentation and research undertaken for the eventual betterment of mankind in general. Whereas in therapeutic experimentation a particular danger to be avoided is that the views or the decisions of others may be permitted to prevail over the actual or carefully presumed decision of the individual, in non-therapeutic research and experimentation a particular danger appears to be that of the individual's own best interests being absorbed into the interests of society as a whole. For the individual's best interests concern not only his physical integrity, but also his intellectual and emotional integrity, and the consequent requirements that, so far as possible, his participation in such research and experimentation should be fully human, and expressed particularly in his informed and free agreement to be a participant.

Access to, or sharing in, all the information relevant to an experimental project may appear to raise two particular difficulties, that of the subject being capable of understanding all the technical complexity involved, and cases where success may be dependent on the subject's being kept in ignorance of his particular contribution to it. In terms of pertinent information adequate to ensure informed decision on the part of the subject, however, it is possible that too much may be made of these difficulties. Minimum and sufficient moral expectations for the potential subject to be enabled to make his decision would be met by his being invited to take part in a project, or a procedure, whose outcome was unknown but would be, if successful, of considerable benefit to others, and whose possible, or likely, effects on him could be reasonably assessed in fairly specific, but non-technical, terms.

Failing such sufficiently candid information, agreement on the part of the potential subject could scarcely be termed free in the sense of being aware of the choices being placed before him. Even given such knowledge, however, and awareness of what would be entailed by a decision to participate, the other major factor in a fully personal decision centres on freedom from any degree of coercion, however subtle or persuasive, and from all undue influence. It would be unrealistic, of course, to ignore the fact that most people in many of their actions act from a number of motives, or from mixed motives, and to demand a kind of clinical purity of free decision which is rarely, if ever, met with in any situation. Nevertheless, particular attention in such cases as we are considering needs to be given to what may be called a 'captive' situation, where the individual, whether by reason of his medical condition or by reason of his social situation, may be at distinct disadvantages which can unduly influence his decision and diminish the amount of freedom which is available to him. The patient in hospital, for instance, is in a particularly vulnerable situation, not only because his physical resources are weak and his mental powers of attention and concentration not at their best, perhaps through medication, and not only because his sheer physical immobility and posture may place him in a further position of subordination to others, but particularly because, in an alien environment which is no more than the ordinary place of work to others, he is, or may consider that he is, heavily dependent on the approval or disapproval of those more knowledgeable and more powerful than he.

Likewise, even in the case of subjects in good health, it is possible for their environment and situation to exert an undue influence on their freedom of choice and freedom to decline to participate. Medical students, again dependent on the approval of superiors, may be considered at risk of manipulation, while more obviously captive populations, such as prison inmates in various countries, may be additionally subjected to various forms of inducement or reward to mitigate the rigour of their pattern of life by agreeing to participate, in a way in which they would not act were they not thus recompensed.

In all such cases, it appears, a fundamental respect for individuals and their capacity for free choice requires that scrupulous attention be paid to avoiding any reality or appearance of undue influence; and this in turn implies that the fundamental relationship between principals and subjects engaged in non-therapeutic research and experimentation should be that of equality as between partners in a joint project. What the researcher has to contribute to such a partnership is his expertise, experience and other resources, but what the subject has to contribute is at least as important, not only for others but also for himself personally, whether it be his time and attention, his health or his state of ill-health (thus turning this latter to positive and constructive account), or his very freedom and willingness. Unwilling or unwitting contributions to research have the effect of diminishing the personhood of the subject, whereas the opportunity for generous and even heroic personal collaboration in seeking further alleviations of man's ills can not only enhance the person but, for the believer, give expression to that love of neighbour in effective terms which sums up so much of the Judaeo-Christian ethic.

If freedom to dispose of one's self in decisions as one thinks right in view of all the pertinent information available is of such importance in the use of subjects for non-therapeutic research and experimentation, then a particular difficulty arises over recourse to subjects who are not in a position so to make their own free decision. And this appears as an acute dilemma in the case of such research on young children. Without some possibility of testing various treatments and dosages on some young persons it does not appear how medical care for that sector of the population can make progress responsibly. And yet, if one adheres to a strong line on the necessity for free and informed consent on the part of the participant, such testing is ruled out of court. No doubt one could involve a general principle of the common good as justifying a disregarding of the need for consent in such cases, but this appears a dangerous line to take in isolation from any other factors, and much harm has been, and can be, perpetrated on individuals in the name of the common good. No doubt also it is relevant to distinguish ethically, apart from what may count in law as an offence against the person, between comparatively trivial procedures with little pain and no after-effects, such as blood-sampling, and others which may carry with them a degree of risk as well as greater and perhaps prolonged discomfort. It also appears desirable, however, not just to leave a vacuum in the place which personal consent would normally occupy, but to attempt in some manner to fill in a form of presumed consent as an additional moral criterion in evaluating non-therapeutic procedures on such subjects. In the nature of the case, such consent cannot be interpretative, as it might be in adults who have become insensible through accident, sickness or old age, as we have already considered. It would have to be constructive consent, in terms of what any rational person would reasonably consider the right action to take in such circumstances, even if this appears unsatisfactory in seeming to put an adult mind into a child's body.

The obvious danger in such a process is that of eliciting

generosity, or even heroism, by proxy, or of imposing altruism on others, on the grounds that this is what they would wish were they in a position to make a decision. It appears essential, therefore, that in such matters a clear distinction should be maintained between what is considered morally obligatory, and to which a child might be constructively considered to give consent as reasonable behaviour, and what is morally desirable as an object of generous consent entailing some measure of self-sacrifice, which cannot lightly be presumed of every human being. In the circumstances, the views of parents and legal guardians are obviously of great importance, but even these might well need to be supplemented and at times weighted in favour of the interests of the child by independent representation on ethical committees, particularly if the child is housed in an institution. The whole matter, both the dilemma of necessary experimentation on children and lines towards a responsible solution, is well expressed in the Proposed International Guidelines of the World Health Organisation and the Council for International Organisations of Medical Sciences, which refine the Revised Helsinki Declaration on biomedical research by observing that

... there are many individuals, including children, adults who are mentally ill or defective, and those who are totally unfamiliar with modern medical concepts, who are incapable of giving adequate consent and from whom consent implies a passive and uncomprehending participation. For such groups, in particular, independent ethical review is imperative.[5]

Helsinki II itself points out that 'medical progress is based on research which ultimately must rest in part on experimentation involving human subjects'.[6] What we have attempted to do in this chapter is explore the nature and aims of such research and experimentation in medicine, and the scientific and ethical values which both beckon them forward and circumscribe their exercise. To expand the human in a human manner may well be finally considered the challenge with which medical science is continuously faced, not least by religious belief. In our final chapter we shall turn to more specifically religious considerations, and their implications for the medical practitioner who is also a believer, and who may be considered to exemplify in himself the continuing dialogue between his professional discipline and his personal belief.

5

Belief and Medicine in Dialogue

In what must be considered the deepest and most detailed attempt of any Christian body to initiate a positive dialogue between religious belief and contemporary society, the bishops of the Second Vatican Council began by affirming their belief that religious faith casts a fresh light on all things by showing them against God's calling of all mankind and by directing the mind towards fully human solutions to all of life's problems.[1] By adopting such a starting point for its considerations the Council was officially ushering in for the Church a new programme of Christian humanism, which would take human reality with all respect and seriousness and explore its strengths and its weaknesses in the strong belief that God, the originator of all worldly and human realities, wishes them to find their own fulfilment.

The theme was not new in Christian thinking although the emphasis was, in its application to a society which, the Council acknowledged, was embarked on changes and developments quite unique in history. In past centuries, much religious thought and reflection had stressed the idea of man's being progressively elevated and divinised by God's grace to become god-like and share in God's own nature. A companion strand of thought, however, had directed attention to God's work in man as making him increasingly human in accordance with God's intentions. This way of viewing God's enterprise for mankind has the merit of starting from human reality as it is to be found, and of considering its inherent potential to become increasingly humanised, by contrast with any other view which might appear to imply an effacement of the human as it is overlaid or subsumed into the divine. By highlighting this 'humanist' approach, the Vatican Council, and much of contemporary religious reflection in general, is not thereby closed in on itself, as if humanity was all. Rather, it espouses an 'open' humanism, which of set purpose begins with human life and experience but is aware of the latent promise in all that is human and is concerned to identify it and bring it to its full flourishing. Thus, Christian humanism will walk side by side with purely secular and other forms of humanism, as setting out from a shared starting point, but it will also be forever encouraging other humanisms to lengthen their stride and to take those extra steps towards the full perfection of which man is capable, and towards the form of human society which alone can do full justice to man who is also the image of God.

Christian humanism, then, is not just a tactic for the Churches to win converts or, in more theological terms, a mere preparation for the Gospel, like breaking up the ground as a prelude to sowing the divine seed which will grow into a full crop although unhappily intermixed with purely human weeds and tares. It is a belief that the human is part of the Gospel, that God's grace is secretly present in the whole of his creation and that his concern is centred on the human person in all its dignity, mystery and destiny. And such a belief finds its expression in the identification by Vatican II of the obligation incumbent on all Christians 'to work with all men in constructing a more human world'.[2] Collaboration of such a kind, however, particularly in advancing human wellbeing and in enhancing the importance and dignity of the human person, must of its very nature be a two-way process, of listening as much as of addressing. It signals the abdication of all claims to possess a monopoly of truth, and the acknowledgement of the universal validity in the statement of one of Christian thought's greatest explorers, Thomas Aquinas, that 'every truth, no matter who utters it, comes from the Holy Spirit'. It lays down, in other words, the ground-rules for dialogue between belief and culture, and in the context of this study it establishes procedures for the possible mutual enrichment of religious belief and medical science. It does not, of course, blur the distinction, but on the contrary enhances the peculiar contributions of belief and medicine, and in particular it respects the autonomy and integrity of medical science. Nevertheless, where the need for increasing specialisation is a prerequisite for any scientific progress, and where, by contrast, religion is at pains to present a unifying vision of man and his destiny in common with his fellows, while belief can continually call for a holistic view of the person and of society, medicine for its part can offer correction by stressing the particular, the bodily and emotional as well as the spiritual components of man and the fact that Christ's saving victory for all men was not only over human sin but also over human suffering, pain and death.

The potential for such dialogue between belief and medicine exists in its richest form in the individual medical practitioner who is also a believer. And for such this intimate interchange brings particular moral responsibilities, which are not simply limited to invoking religious considerations to enforce professional duties of competence, truthfulness, loyalty, and the like, but are also concerned with how professional experience in turn questions and probes religious beliefs and the moral conclusions to which they may appear to lead. In the previous chapter we considered the choices facing all specialists, in their personal as in their professional lives, and the sacrifices which they may be willing to make in pursuit of their chosen goals. For the believer, one such sacrifice which cannot be made in favour of any other consideration is that of his belief, not simply in the sense of abandoning religious belief, but of so compartmentalising it in his mind as to render it atrophied and ineffective, even when accompanied by such religious performances as worship and church attendance. The danger for the believer, as the Old Testament prophets and Jesus himself warned, has always been to separate and compartmentalise his religious belief from the rest of his life, and to neglect the fact that, if man is at heart a searcher, as we have suggested, then that attitude must also apply to his searching attitude towards his faith and the particular beliefs in which this finds expression. If such a fearless approach to personal belief does not accompany personal and professional progress or enquiry in other areas of his mind, then an unhealthy imbalance is set up which can result in belief remaining, not child-like, but childish and infantile. And if such belief is then subjected to strain from other more mature, or adult, areas of the mind, as it so often can be today, then it is in danger of being dismissed or abandoned on grounds of what may be claimed as intellectual honesty, or of becoming purely conventional in its routine expression in worship. What is more, the other and more adult areas of the mind are then also deprived of the challenge and enrichment which a less immature religious belief could provide and contribute.

Such personal enquiry of an adult nature into one's beliefs can be termed theology, although for many the word smacks more of academic, in more than one sense, exercises and esoteric studies. In a more attractive expression, the Christian thinker, Anselm of Canterbury, wrote of 'faith seeking understanding', and it is in that more natural, and even more ordinary, sense that the challenge which exists increasingly for all today can be best expressed. It is, if we may so express it, a matter of trying to make faith-sense of experience and at the same time of making experience-sense of faith; of finding an overall context of a meaning and purpose to life within which to locate all our ordinary experiences and interrelate them, and at the same time of continually checking such a vision of life against each new experience as it arises. This dialectical activity of submitting experience to the bar of belief and of submitting belief to the bar of experience is increasingly today a requirement of every believer, on pain of leaving his experience unanchored and his belief unsubstantiated.

For the believer who is at home in the rapidly and dramatically expanding world of medical science, such a personal dialogue is not only an urgent invitation to him individually, if he is to avoid living in a state of spiritual schizophrenia. It is also a unique expert contribution which he can make both to his scientific community and to his religious community. As such, it is a demanding dialogue for him personally, since it can exemplify in his own religious and professional living the tensions which must arise at times between belief and medicine. In the course of these chapters we have explored some of the major issues in which medical advances and religious belief can address each other in their joint pursuit of human wholeness, and within this context we have considered such fundamental questions as the origin of life, its purpose and its destiny through death. In addition to these far-reaching considerations there are for the medical practitioner others of a perhaps more practical and everyday import which can be appropriately considered here in terms of the conscience of the believing practitioner in contemporary society.

One of the most celebrated, and perhaps least understood, of the sayings of Jesus was his advice to those who tried to trap him with a trick question over payment of taxes to the Roman occupying power: 'Render to Caesar the things that are Caesar's, and to God the things that are God's' (Mk 12:17). What did it mean then, and what can it mean today? The payment of Roman taxes was a perpetual and humiliating reminder to a proud people of their subjection to Rome. And, to add blasphemy to injury, the Roman coinage in which taxes had to be paid bore something which was equally hateful to the Jewish people, a graven image, that of the head of the divinised emperor Tiberius. It might be, however, that by skilful questioning about this contentious issue it would be possible to neutralise this Jesus who was showing himself such an outspoken critic of the religious establishment. Perhaps he could be drawn into a damaging statement against the occupying powers, or alternatively be forced to preach to his fellow-Jews a duty to collaborate with the Roman imperialists.

In one sense Jesus may be thought to have evaded with equal skill the trick question of principle put to him, 'Is it lawful to pay taxes to Caesar or not?', by reducing it to the tiny particular of a Roman shilling which, like all coinage, was the Emperor's property. 'If it's his, then give it to him.' But perhaps there is also a much deeper meaning to this part of his answer, one which would have been of critical importance to the early Christian community as it developed and spread within the Roman Empire and had to consider what its relationship could be, or should be, to the powerful pagan culture in which it struggled for survival. And perhaps also it is a teaching which is of permanent relevance to the Churches in what may be fast becoming a post-Christian culture. A coin, as symbolising an effective system of exchange, is the expression of a network of economic cooperation, and of some measure of agreed stability and social order. From this point of view, then, the gesture of Jesus may be seen as symbolic, recognising that Roman rule had given to the mediterranean world, including his own country, undoubted benefits of peace and prosperity, of law and social order, upon which the Christian church also was heavily dependent in exercising its world-wide mission. And such benefits in their turn entailed corresponding social obligations on the part of all who enjoyed them.

But, of course, as so often in replying to questions, Jesus did not leave the matter there. His agenda was never just that set by his questioners and his critics; and he always went far beyond, aiming to open their eyes, expand their concerns, and lift their sights. Ritual washing before meals? Be clean in heart. Who is your neighbour? Whoever needs you. Forgive seven times? Seventy times seven. Pay taxes to Caesar? Give God *his* due. And so, 'Render to Caesar the things that are Caesar's – and to God the things that are God's.' It would be a misunderstanding of this saying of Jesus to take it as teaching that some matters come under the civil government, and other matters come under God, as if he were identifying two distinct areas of competence, and providing a basis for some doctrine of due separation of church and state, declaring some areas of our lives as outside, or outwith, the claims of God. His argument is not one which separates, but one which accumulates. If there are some areas of our lives where society, or the state, can have legitimate claims upon us, it is even more the case that God, in whose image and likeness we are made (as the coin was in that of Tiberius), has claims upon the whole of our lives, and in every area of our activity, whether personal, social or professional.

What this teaching addresses, then, to medical practitioners who are also believers is the acknowledgement that it is part of their human and Christian vocation to respond conscientiously to the needs of individuals in society, and to the claims of others upon their services, knowledge and judgement, subject only to any overriding claims which God may be considered to make upon them. Such claims of God, however, are not to be seen as opaque commands issuing from divine authority. They arise from, and are rooted in, the life, activity, death and resurrection of Christ himself, who can be seen as devoting himself utterly to bringing back to God 'the things that are God's'. This he did not in the mere material sense of restoring possessions to their rightful owner, but in terms of bringing his Father's love to all men, and so bringing all men to the healing embrace of their Father's love. Throughout his life's ministry we find him continually healing, comforting and strengthening the sick in body, mind and soul. In his words and his astonishing actions he was not just making claims for God's universal lordship and proving that he himself was more than human. He was spreading among men even during his lifetime the victory over sickness and death which his own death and resurrection would achieve definitively, and which his followers would be called upon to communicate in the years to come. All Christians, then, whose faith is founded on the rock of Christ's resurrection, and whose hope is in a resurrection of all men to eternal life with Christ in God, have a share in Christ's own ministry of healing, as the power of his saving death and resurrection works itself out through them in human history. And in that ministry of bringing healing to all God's beloved sons and daughters, medical science and the medical professions have a particular and privileged place and vocation.

To be thus called to, or engaged in, Christ's healing service to humanity may bring to those engaged in medicine a deep sense of satisfaction, however mixed it may be at times with disappointments, sadness and frustrations. It must also, however, bring many perplexities and challenges for the believer who wishes to be as sure as he can that the ministry of healing which he offers to his fellow-men is indeed that of Christ, particularly when he is working in a society and among colleagues who to a significant degree may not share his beliefs or their practical applications. St Paul acknowledged to his fellow-Christians in pagan Corinth that it was not required of them to dissociate themselves from those who did not share their beliefs or behaviour (1 Cor 5:10), and indeed such an exclusive withdrawal from society would be a negation of the interior dynamic of the Christian gospel. Nevertheless, it raises particular difficulties for all Christians, including those engaged in many of the modern professions, of teasing out what might be considered rules for association with others in a predominantly non-Christian society, when such association involves actions at variance with Christian beliefs.

To meet such situations traditional moral theology elaborated certain practical principles relating to 'cooperation' in the sin of another, which may be seen, not so much as principles automatically delivering moral answers, but more as instruments for moral analysis of the situation. The first is intended to clear the ground, by affirming that when one willingly and knowingly collaborates with others who are equally bent on wrong-doing, then one is acting as immorally as the other principals in the action. The real problems begin to emerge, however, when one's contribution to the actions of others cannot be described as that of a willing accomplice, but rather of a more or less unwilling accomplice. How is one to assess morally the situation where one allows one's self to be taken advantage of, where there is nothing morally exceptionable about what one is actually doing, but where one knows that it will be incorporated into another's actions for a purpose with which one cannot agree? Is it possible morally to temper willingness with degrees of reluctance? Such problems are commonplace in every society, whether it involve government use of one's taxes for, say, defence purposes which one finds morally repugnant, or imposition on one's social tolerance to conduct businesses, such as sex shops, which one considers morally exploitative of others' weaknesses, or another individual relying on one's silence or one's loyalty for success in perpetrating some injury on a third party. Within the medical and nursing professions, many individuals who may be opposed to abortion, euthanasia, systematic neglect of newly-born and severely handicapped babies, donor insemination or experimentation on human embryos, or routine sterilisation, may nevertheless find themselves in situations in which they are professionally expected to participate in such procedures, or even in which their ordinary services are being canalised in the direction of such procedures, to a greater or lesser degree.

Somewhat confusingly today, and as a heritage of Aristotelian terminology, moral theology refers to cooperation in such actions when one is wholeheartedly in favour of them as 'formal cooperation', not thereby meaning, as might be expected, cooperation which is 'purely' formal or perfunctory or casual, but cooperative action which is fully expressive of one's complete consent. By contrast, when collaboration can be described as unwilling, or reluctant and grudging, then it is

Pat STEVENS

CHY ARKELD
HOLLY BUSH CLOSE
STEEL NE47 0HE
HEXHAMSHIRE .

Selves a
Youth Employment

referred to as 'material cooperation', in the sense that it does not express, or embody, one's complete consent, but is as raw material adopted by another in order to further his own wrongful purpose. Given that, in such terms, formal cooperation is never justifiable, the question which moral theology proceeds to consider is, under what circumstances, if any, might material, or reluctant, cooperation ever be morally acceptable behaviour? The answer to this question proceeds by two steps, analysing first the degree of involvement in the over-all wrong action which is possessed by one's reluctant contribution, and then for each degree of unwilling complicity considering what might be possible justifying factors. The first step is frequently described in terms of either 'remote' or 'proximate' cooperation, with the rider that the more proximate such (always material) cooperation is, the more difficult it is to justify morally. The language is metaphorical, using the idea of space and nearness to, or farness from, the centre of the action to identify the degree of involvement in that action. And it may be seen aptly exemplified in the judgement of some religious authorities, attempting to provide moral guidance for those hospital personnel who wish to have as little as professionally possible to do with abortions, that they should not participate in what goes on inside the operating theatre but that they might in good conscience continue with their routine duties outside the theatre, including, presumably, preparing the patient for the operation and providing post-operative care.

This particular judgement breaks down, of course, when abortion techniques are simplified, and bedside abortions by drip-mechanism, for instance, are also possible. But what it attempts to provide is a sort of rule-of-thumb guidance in which the underlying thinking about degrees of moral 'proximity' to the centre of the action is expressed in literal degrees of physical proximity. And it is the thinking rather than its physical expression which is the operative moral factor. If, for instance, what underlies it is the consideration that one may continue to provide those services which one normally or routinely does for every patient, regardless of the operation, then it could be argued that even within the theatre and during the abortion itself any 'material' contribution on the part of nursing or medical staff which they would provide in any other operation could be considered to be as justifiable as their contributions on the other side of the theatre door. Other considerations must, of course, also enter into such attempts to shade cooperation of a reluctant nature, in case the metaphorical language of near and far dominates the attempt at moral analysis. It is here that another way of distinguishing material cooperation is sometimes invoked, to identify degrees of immediacy in one's contribution to the wrongful action. Such a differentiation between 'mediate' and 'immediate' cooperation does not refer to the timing of events but rather to one's degree of instrumentality in the bringing about of the final result. In one sense this may be considered as pointing a difference between cooperation which is essential, such that if it were not forthcoming then the final result could not be achieved, and cooperation which, if not provided, could easily be obtained from another. But primarily it is again an attempt to identify how closely one is involved in the achieving of the final effect.

When traditional moral theology has identified the measure of reluctant cooperation, and therefore of moral responsibility, involved in one's doing what is in itself, or in isolation, morally irreproachable, or even morally praiseworthy, it then proceeds to consider what other factors might justify one in permitting others to distort such actions by absorbing them into their own wrongful purposes. Broadly speaking, such possibly compensating factors can be reduced to two: that involving personal hardship should one refuse to cooperate even materially, such as losing a post, either in the present or in prospect, and with it significant means of livelihood; and that which takes into account the amount of greater good one may be able to achieve in other respects. Such good may be seen as more than compensating for the harm in which one is an unwilling participant and without which one might not be in a position to achieve the greater good. In general, this weighing of factors may be regarded by some as coming suspiciously close to making the end justify the means, although this conclusion does not necessarily follow. Others may fear the allurements of rationalisation on the part of individuals, but this also does not invalidate the principles elaborated. Yet others may wonder what is the point of such minute calculations, and either exhort simply to do the best in the circumstances, or more forthrightly conclude that the only line of action for a person of moral principle, especially if a believer committed to giving good example and witness to the values of the Gospel, is to decline to play any part in proceedings which would compromise those values. The fact, however, that the middle way sought by the traditional path of such cooperation which we have sketched can draw fire from both such extremes appears to indicate its strength in attempting to do justice both to the sensitivities of conscience and to the practicalities of life.

In contemporary society, nonetheless, it might be added, there is at least one additional factor which needs to be considered in such cases and which the traditional approach of cooperation in the wrongdoing of another did not appear to take into account: the consideration that the other person may not himself believe he is doing wrong, but that, on the contrary, the action which he envisages may appear morally right, or even morally obligatory, to him. In more general terms, the classical doctrine on cooperation did not make allowance for living in a pluralistic society, where different individuals may differ fundamentally in at least some of the human and moral values which they consider important, and in which tolerance of the views of others, rather than disapproval, is considered morally relevant in all one's own actions. And believers who are uncomfortably aware of a lack of such tolerance in the past or in their religious background, and who feel a particular call in the present to respect the conscientiously held convictions of others, even when, or particularly when, they do not personally share them, may find the traditional doctrine of cooperation not just too nice in its detail but too uncooperative in its lack of appreciation of the views of others. Should not one collaborate to the fullest possible extent with friends or colleagues or even fellow-citizens whose values may be as deeply cherished and respected as one's own?

The difficulty about this approach, which highlights the virtues of tolerance and of not imposing one's own religious or moral beliefs on others by declining to act alongside them, is that tolerance is a two-way street. To the extent that I respect the conscience of others, to that extent I am entitled to have my own conscience treated with respect. It is not a tolerant society in which tolerance is selective. And moral conscience is not really respected if I surrender my own moral convictions in order to help others do what they think right, any more than it is respected if, in order to pursue my own aims, I require others to act against their own deeply held convictions. Tolerance, in other words, is a hard-won virtue which does not entail moral surrender on the part of some and moral supremacy on the part of others. It exists at its best as the mutual respect which lies between those who are equally committed to moral values but who honestly differ in how they view and express such values. As such, it does not commit to action in common, if either would consider this immoral, although it does commit to respect for the other's position and avoidance of behaviour which would actively prevent another from living out his position, unless perhaps the rights and interests of a third party were seen to prevail.

Part of such tolerance in general, finally, which for the believer may require further exploration, is the avoidance of mental intolerance in claiming to possess a monopoly of truth in moral matters, such that any who disagree are either knaves or fools. Even the Roman Catholic Church, which, in such matters, lays the greatest claim to divinely-derived authority, and for all its dogma of teaching infallibly in certain circumstances, cannot point to any piece of its moral teaching and assert its absolute truth in every circumstance as taught infallibly. The issues with which these chapters have been concerned provide a case in point. By the very nature of morality, concerned as it ultimately is with human and contingent variables, it is easier to gain certitude, and agreement, at the level of general principles than it is at the level of more specific principles or of particular situations. Nevertheless, the human moral endeavour, as the enterprise of medical science, finds itself concerned with ultimates in the light of which its day-to-day activities fall to be considered, whether explicitly or implicitly. And it is at the level of such ultimates that religious belief may be consulted with fully justifiable confidence. As the Second Vatican Council observed, Christians' view of the complete vocation of man 'increases the weight of their obligation to work with all men in constructing a more human world'.[3] The Council saw the Church's own contribution to this task as exercised 'most of all by her healing and elevating impact on the dignity of the person, by the way in which she strengthens the seams of human society and imbues the everyday activity of men with a deeper meaning and importance. Thus, through her individual members and her whole community, the Church believes she can contribute greatly toward making the family of man and its history more human'.[4] And when it comes to defining the human, the Council stresses 'a view of the whole human person, a view in which the values of intellect, will, conscience, and fraternity are pre-eminent'.[5]

With its sights fixed on such values, with which, perhaps, few individuals would be found to disagree, religious belief can explore in the contingent realities of life how they may find expression in moral choices and behaviour. It is here, however, where facts and their interpretation, and conflicts of values, enter into the picture, that there is much more room for disagreement, debate and error, particularly in an increasingly complex universe. Moreover, as the Council recognised, many of the scientific and other developments of modern society can 'raise new questions which influence life and demand new theological investigations'.[6] And perhaps no developments in our contemporary world more exemplify this raising of new questions and demand for new theological investigation than those concerned with life itself. In such theological investigation into the origin and destiny of the human person, and into the relationships between persons which will most express that 'more human world' to which the Church is committed by the Gospel, it would be a serious impoverishment to consider it the preserve of professional theologians alone. In the attempt to relate belief and experience, as we have described theology, there can be no substitute for the active presence and contribution of those most experienced in the life-sciences. If these chapters have had some effect in stimulating members of the medical professions as well as others, whether to agreement or to disagreement of a reasonable nature, they will have made some contribution to the dialogue between belief and bio-ethics which, the author believes, is of such importance not only for belief and for science, but for the future of humanity in our society. In any case, the dialogue between bio-ethics and belief must be pursued, in order to bring an even deeper awareness of what really constitutes that love of neighbour, or quest for human betterment, upon which each is engaged. Belief may say it must not be too earthbound or pragmatic, while medicine may reply it cannot be too celestial or a priori. Belief will encourage medical science to pursue knowledge and truth, but to encompass them with love and other necessary limitations; science may test that love and in its turn question those limitations, encouraging belief to explore them in what the Council termed 'new theological investigations'. If they can, in dialogue, so pursue truth in its various manifestations and implications, then neither the one nor the other will be far from the kingdom of God or his design for the work of his hands.

Notes

Introduction

1 *Encyclopedia of Bioethics* (ed. Warren T. Reich), vol. I, Macmillan, 1978, p. xix.

Chapter 1: *Human Fertility Control*

1 Cf. *AAS*, 41 (1949), pp. 559–560; 43 (1951), pp. 849–851; 48 (1956), pp. 470–474.
2. W. Walters and P. Singer (edd.), *Test-Tube Babies*, Oxford, 1982, p. 40.
3 Encyclical Letter *Humanae Vitae*, par. 13; *AAS*, 60 (1968), p. 489.
4 Apostolic Exhortation *Familiaris Consortio*, Catholic Truth Society, London, 1981, par. 31.
5 *British Medical Journal*, 20th November 1982, p. 1480.
6 March 1983, Section 14 (Legal Aspects), para. 3, 1.
7 *Ibid.*, para. 4, 6; 4, 1.

Chapter 2: *Death and Dying*

1 *Cadaveric Organs for Transplantation*. A Code of Practice including the Diagnosis of Brain Death, London, 1983.
2 *The Times*, 3rd February 1975. *British Medical Journal*, 1975, 1, pp. 251–255.
3 *AAS*, 49 (1957), pp. 1031, 1033.
4 *Euthanasia and Clinical Practice: trends, principles and alternatives*, The Linacre Centre, London, 1982, p. 74.
5 Cf. *ibid.*, pp. 85–88.

Chapter 3: *The Beginning of Life*

1 Encyclical Letter *Casti Connubii*, par. 63; *AAS*, 22 (1930), p. 563.
2 *AAS* 43 (1951), p. 838.
3 *Historia Animalium*, VII, 3; 583^{b}, 2–23 (trans. D. W. Thompson, Oxford, 1910).
4 Aquinas, *In III Sententiarum*, dist. 3, q. 5, art. 2.
5 Aquinas, *De anima*, art. 11.
6 *Summa Theologiae*, Pars IIIa, q. 33, art. 1.
7 *The Church in the Modern World*, no. 51. Cf. W. M. Abbott

(ed.), *The Documents of Vatican II*, Chapman, 1966, pp. 255–256.

8 In J. T. Noonan, Jr (ed.), *The Morality of Abortion*, Cambridge, Mass, 1970, p. 46, n. 158.

9 Sacred Congregation for the Doctrine of the Faith, *Declaration on Abortion*, no. 7; *AAS*, 66 (1974) p. 734.

10 *Ibid.*, note 19; *AAS*, p. 738.

11 *Ibid.*, no. 13; *AAS, ibid.*

12 *Ibid.*, no. 13; note 19; *AAS, ibid.*

13 *Ibid.*

14 *Ibid.*

15 Supra, p. 39.

16 *Theological Studies*, 31 (1970), pp. 76–105.

17 *Liber ecclesiasticorum dogmatum*, cap. 14; Migne, *Patrologia latina*, vol. 58, col. 984. Cf. Lombard, *Liber II Sententiarum*, dist. XVIII, cap. VII.

18 Encyclical Letter *Humani Generis*, no. 36; *AAS* 42 (1950), p. 575.

19 Pierre Teilhard de Chardin, *The Phenomenon of Man*, Collins, 1963, p. 165.

20 *Ibid.*, p. 180.

21 Cf. *ibid.*, p. 29.

22 Karl Rahner, *Hominisation. The Evolutionary Origin of Man as a Theological Problem*, Burns and Oates, 1965, p. 94.

23 *Ibid.*, pp. 55, 58.

24 *Ibid.*, p. 92.

25 *Ibid.*, pp. 98–99.

26 *Ibid.*, pp. 95–96.

27 *Ibid.*, p. 99.

28 *Declaration on Abortion*, note 19; no. 13; *AAS*, 66 (1974), pp. 738–739.

29 *Ibid.*, no. 13; *AAS*, p. 739.

30 *Ibid.*, note 19; *AAS*, p. 738.

31 de Chardin, *op. cit.*, p. 165.

32 Supra, p. 60.

Chapter 4: *Medical Research and Experimentation*

1 *British Medical Journal*, 20th November 1982, p. 1480.

2 Supra, p. 60.

3 *AAS*, 75 (1983), pp. 35–39.

4 Supra, p. 33.